COMPLETE
DUTCH
OVEN
COOKBOOK

COMPLETE DUTCH OVEN COOKBOOK

105 RECIPES FOR YOUR MOST VERSATILE POT

Katie Hale

ROCKRIDGE
PRESS

For general information on our other products and services or to obtain technical support, please contact our Customer Care Department within the United States at (866) 744-2665, or outside the United States at (510) 253-0500.

Rockridge Press publishes its books in a variety of electronic and print formats. Some content that appears in print may not be available in electronic books, and vice versa.

Interior and Cover Designer: Richard Tapp
Art Producer: Megan Baggot
Editor: Maxine Marshall
Production Editor: Matthew Burnett
Production Manager: Riley Hoffman

Cover photography ©Marija Vidal, Cameron Whitman/Stocksy, Nadine Greeff/Stocky; Evi Abeler, ii, vi, 32, 152; Nadine Greeff, x, 108; Mary Ellen Bartley/StockFood USA, 14; Gemma Comas/StockFood USA, 48; Cameron Whitman/Stocksy, 60, 93, 122; Marija Vidal, 76; The Picture Pantry/StockFood USA, 138.

Paperback ISBN: 978-1-64876-485-1
eBook ISBN: 978-1-63807-972-9
R0

TO THE STRONGEST WOMEN I KNOW: RITA,

STEPHANIE, CATHY, AND MEGAN

CONTENTS

INTRODUCTION

From the smell of my mom's pot roast slow cooking in the oven on Sunday to Granny's peach cobbler, the kitchen has always brought me joy. When I was young, my family enjoyed being in the kitchen preparing meals, often throwing in a "secret" ingredient that everyone claimed made the food better.

I was inspired by them, and my love for cooking continued to develop into my teen and young adult years as I began watching renowned chefs on television. I was soon learning techniques, finding out how flavors blended, and discovering that quality ingredients made a difference. The result was a passion for food and cooking that has stayed with me for life.

In 2010, I decided to take that love of cooking online by working on food and recipe blogs, where I continue to hone my skills. It was during this time of food exploration that my sister introduced me to the Dutch oven.

The result of that fateful meeting was a newfound joy for preparing not only basic stews and soups, but also all manner of meals in my Dutch oven. In time, my Dutch oven soon took pride of place on my stovetop as that *one* pan—the one used so often it never gets put away. Because of its multiple uses, I am here to show you that a Dutch oven is so much more than a good-looking soup pot!

Here are just a few things that the Dutch oven excels at: It consistently holds heat when slowly cooking a tough piece of meat in the oven. It's the ideal vessel for making my mama's Classic Corn Bread (page 37), which pairs perfectly with a rich chili (prepared earlier in the same pot). Delicious desserts like my granny's classic Fresh Peach Cobbler (page 146) turn out even better than usual when prepared in the Dutch oven, as the lid keeps the crust from burning. Of course, it was preparing the classic holiday Prime Rib of Beef (page 134) in the Dutch oven that sealed the deal: This would be my favorite kitchen tool.

I decided to write the *Complete Dutch Oven Cookbook* to help fellow Dutch oven enthusiasts (and soon-to-be enthusiasts) explore the range and versatility of this incredible pot. Not only can you create tender, slow-cooked meals in the Dutch oven, but it also excels at preparing staple items like homemade Chicken Bone Broth (page 154). In your Dutch oven, a batch of dried beans takes on rich flavor. I love the ability to make fluffy rice to pair with any meal, all while knowing that my spicy Red Lentil Spinach Curry (page 82) can be cooked in just 35 minutes. It turns out, using the Dutch oven makes mealtime easier than ever.

I am excited to share my favorite recipes with you as well as techniques for cooking with the Dutch oven. Follow along as I divulge all of my best tips, and some additional resources, to make using your Dutch oven easy and satisfying. Let's begin!

1

THE MOST COMPLETE POT IN YOUR KITCHEN

The Dutch oven is a beloved classic, but there are many ways to use this versatile pot. I'll share with you the best ways to clean and care for your Dutch oven, how to cook with it on the stovetop, and when to use it in the oven for best results. I'm even including a list of pantry essentials to help as you experiment with recipes in your Dutch oven.

This cookbook is designed to give you tips for use and showcase a variety of meals and cooking techniques, including baking, braising, roasting, searing, and slow cooking.

ONE VERSATILE VESSEL

Every chef, whether home cook or professional, has a few tools they reach for regularly. In my kitchen, the Dutch oven is right next to my chef's knife as the most commonly used item. One reason for this is the pot's versatility—there is so much you can do with it.

The first thing to know about using a Dutch oven is that it produces even cooking better than a typical pot. Its design allows the surface to hold a regulated temperature more efficiently than other vessels. This feature is what makes the Dutch oven ideal for slow-cooking stews, braising meat, and slow-roasting meat and vegetable dishes.

When using the Dutch oven on the stovetop, you will find that your foods cook evenly, and because the pot holds heat better, foods cook faster without burning as easily. In the oven, you have the option of cooking with or without the lid, offering a way to hold in flavor and moisture while keeping the temperature even. When braising meats, you are given a chance to seal in that flavor on the stovetop, then move the food right into the oven so no flavor or heat is lost in the cooking process.

Because the Dutch oven is typically made with a cast-iron base, it is sturdy and long lasting. A Dutch oven is a wonderful investment that can be used for your needs, then passed down to future generations. Today, most Dutch ovens are enamel coated, and that is what I used for the recipes in this book.

KNOW YOUR DUTCH OVEN

A large pot with a fancy name can be intimidating, but it is a wonderful tool, and I'm confident you will find that a Dutch oven replaces other cookware and makes your cooking experience easier and more satisfying. It is worth taking time to get to know your Dutch oven. Learning its unique properties can offer even experienced cooks more freedom and confidence to use this tool daily. The following tips can also serve as a handy guide should you decide to invest in additional Dutch ovens to add to your kitchen cookware arsenal.

Size and Shape

Dutch ovens come in a variety of sizes, and though the recipes in this cookbook are designed for a 5½-quart Dutch oven, that size is not the only choice that will suit your needs.

Dutch ovens are available in sizes as small as 1 quart—ideal for preparing 1 or 2 servings—all the way to the 13¼-quart capacity, capable of holding upwards of 10 servings. Although the 1-quart Dutch oven is popular as a decorative serving dish, it is best suited for whipping up sauces or gravies. The most common sizes for general-use cooking are the 3-quart Dutch oven, which holds enough food to serve 3 or 4, the 5½-quart pot that can serve 4 to 6, and the 7-quart option that serves 6 to 8.

Dutch ovens come in both oval and round shapes. The traditional round Dutch oven is most popular and best for stovetop recipes. The oval Dutch oven is an excellent choice for anything baked but does not work quite as well on the stovetop because the oval shape usually means that the whole pot cannot sit on a single burner. Many bakers prefer their bread to look loaf-like (and less round), and thus opt for an oval-shaped Dutch oven. The longer, oval shape is also great for preparing large turkeys or chickens. That said, both shapes can function well in your kitchen and are interchangeable, in most cases.

Material and Coating

In addition to varying in shape and size, Dutch ovens are also made using different materials. Although most Dutch ovens are made with a cast-iron base, there are some aluminum and ceramic varieties available. These aluminum and ceramic pots are often called "French ovens," and although they are durable and shaped similarly to a cast-iron Dutch oven with a sealing lid, they do not hold heat as well as cast iron does.

Cast-iron Dutch ovens are sometimes left uncoated, and sometimes sealed with an enamel coating. The traditional uncoated cast-iron Dutch oven is a great choice for those who may not only want to use their pot in their home kitchen, but also when cooking over an open flame. An uncoated cast-iron Dutch oven can be used in hot coals, over a campfire, or inside a wood stove. The potential downside to a solid cast-iron Dutch oven is that it retains flavors and smells from past meals (like a cast-iron skillet will), and the material has the potential to rust if not cared for properly.

Enamel-coated cast-iron Dutch ovens have benefits in the kitchen and can be very beautiful. Not only are these sometimes brightly colored pots aesthetically pleasing to look at, but they are easy to clean with soap and water. You will also find that the enamel-coated options do not rust or retain flavors or smells from past meals.

The Lid

All Dutch ovens come with a well-fitting lid. Not only is the fit important, but most enamel-coated Dutch ovens have ridges or spikes on the inside of the lid. This allows the lid to help return moisture in the pot or food being cooked. In essence, the lid acts as a baster for the food. If the lid on your Dutch oven does not fit well, contact the manufacturer for a replacement.

If you have an uncoated cast-iron Dutch oven and are interested in accessories for outdoor cooking, you can find attachments anywhere that sells camping equipment and supplies.

Brand and Budget Considerations

The most widely used brands of Dutch ovens include Cuisinart, Le Creuset, Lodge, and the less-expensive brands available on Amazon. Each has its benefits and price point, depending on your needs.

The most common brand and model, with the overall best reviews, is the enamel-coated Le Creuset Dutch oven. At the time of writing, this model cost between $300 and $400 for the 5½-quart model. The Cuisinart enamel-coated Dutch oven is a more affordable option, at $80 to $100 for the 5½-quart pot. If you want the ability to use your Dutch oven both indoors and outdoors, the Lodge solid cast-iron Dutch oven costs around $50 for a pre-seasoned 5-quart version.

WHY IS IT CALLED A DUTCH OVEN?

The modern Dutch oven is not actually native to the Netherlands, but it was, indeed, inspired by the Dutch method of casting brass for cookware. The method was observed by Englishman Abraham Darby in 1707, which he brought back to his mill, where, through trial and error, he found he could cast lower-cost iron in sand to create cookware more affordably.

The term "Dutch oven" was then coined as the method of creating cast-iron lidded pots. Over hundreds of years of Dutch, English, and American history, the actual cookware has changed slightly. It's most commonly used to describe the thick-walled, deep cast-iron pot with a tight lid and an enamel coating.

In times of chuck wagons, beloved during the western expansion of the United States in the 1880s, the cast-iron Dutch oven grew in popularity, and its tradition of use carries over today, with many using it in regular everyday food preparation.

CARING FOR YOUR DUTCH OVEN

The Dutch oven, although larger than most kitchen pots and pans, is one of the easiest to clean. Because I primarily use an enamel-coated Dutch oven, I simply wipe any food debris from the surface with a damp cloth and hand wash the pot and lid in hot soapy water. Sometimes, I will place it in the dishwasher on the normal wash setting. This next section walks you through some basic guidelines for treating and cleaning your Dutch oven, whether it is enamel-coated or uncoated cast iron, and includes a few tips and things to keep in mind as you go.

Enamel-Coated Cast Iron

The enamel coating on a Dutch oven is beneficial because it allows you to clean your Dutch oven more easily. It is almost always safe to wash your enamel-coated Dutch oven in the dishwasher, or it can be cleaned by hand with hot water and soap.

Food that sticks onto the coating can be scraped off easily with a rubber spatula or scraper. You can also add hot water to the pot, bring it to a boil, and boil for 5 minutes to loosen the stuck-on food, then use a spatula to scrape it off the pot. Make sure, whether cooking or cleaning, that you do not use any metal utensils on your pot, as they will damage the coating and potentially mix it into the food.

To dry your enamel-coated Dutch oven, wipe it with a dry cloth, or let it air-dry (with the lid off) until completely dry.

Uncoated Cast Iron

The uncoated cast-iron Dutch oven needs additional care when cleaning it. As your pot has a seasoned cast-iron coating, do not use soap to wash the pot. Use hot water and a clean, damp cloth to wipe any food from the surface.

Just as you should not use soap on an uncoated cast-iron pot, do not place it in the dishwasher, either. This will remove the seasoning (the quality that makes cast iron a nonstick surface) and will require you to go through the seasoning process again.

When caring for your Dutch oven, check the manufacturer's recommendations as some brands have special care instructions. For example, some generic brands of Dutch ovens have a Teflon nonstick coating, rather than the traditional cast iron or enamel-coated cast iron. In those instances, it is extra important to follow the brand-specific recommendations for cleaning the Dutch oven.

COOKING WITH YOUR DUTCH OVEN

The Dutch oven truly is a versatile piece of cookware. Great food textures, even heat distribution, and the ability to cook large items are some of the qualities that make Dutch ovens unique. Classic dishes often prepared in a Dutch oven include pot roasts, stews, and breads. However, the Dutch oven also makes a delicious peach cobbler, or even a creamy risotto. Whether you are braising, frying, roasting, or stewing, the Dutch oven is a wonderful go-to tool for preparing meals.

Steam and Boil

Any food you would normally steam or boil in a soup pot can be prepared flavorfully in your Dutch oven. It is ideal for preparing side dishes, like boiling potatoes for mashed potatoes or cooking fluffy rice perfectly every time. Recipes like Creamy Mashed Potatoes (page 55) showcase this cooking technique.

Sear, Sauté, and Fry

Your Dutch oven is designed to sear, sauté, and fry a variety of foods perfectly. This feature is part of what makes this tool so useful in the kitchen. Challenge yourself to go further with the Dutch oven—use it to sauté vegetables or sear meats before topping them with liquid and seasonings. Then, it's easy to bring the food to a simmer, cover the pot, and let it all cook slowly, building rich flavors. My favorite cooking method for using the Dutch oven is to sear a nice steak on the stovetop, then finish it in the oven. The pot's deep sides also make it ideal for frying foods without a mess, allowing for even oil coverage of whatever you are cooking. Try Bacon-Fried Brussels Sprouts (page 50) and Sautéed Garlic Kale with Red Peppers (page 57) to take your veggie game to new levels.

Simmer, Braise, and Stew

Simmering, braising, and stewing foods is easier than ever when you have the even heat distribution the Dutch oven provides. You can use your pot to simmer risotto for a delicious side dish, stew pork and root vegetables for a complete meal, or braise your favorite meats to ultimate tenderness.

The Dutch oven's tight-fitting lid makes braising meats much easier to manage. In fact, the best beef roast you will make is one that has been seared on the stovetop to seal in flavor, then covered and slowly braised in the oven. Try the Sirloin Tips with Mushroom Gravy (page 129) or Tomato Basil Braised Chicken (page 111) to see what I mean.

Roast and Broil

I have found that preparing meals in the oven with my Dutch oven has made mealtimes much easier and more predictable. With its thick walls and the even heat that the Dutch oven provides, I know my food will cook evenly and beautifully every time.

Most recipes I choose to prepare in the oven are those that need extended cook times or that benefit from sealing in moisture while cooking. From a simple baked beans side dish to braised chicken thighs, like the Braised Cajun Chicken Leg Quarters (page 110), you'll find that the oven works wonderfully for many of your favorite recipes as well as a few new ones you can add to your repertoire.

Bake

One of the best parts of having a Dutch oven is that you can bake so many items with it. It's ideal for making biscuits, breads, cakes, cobblers, rolls, and even cheesecake. Anything you could bake in another dish can be baked in your Dutch oven. As you might expect, the dessert recipes in this book showcase the Dutch oven's fabulous baking abilities. Try the Baked Apple Dumplings (page 140) for a sweet treat and experiment with fun recipes like Flaky Buttermilk Biscuits (page 38) and Parmesan Pesto Bread (page 42).

YOU CAN COOK WITH YOUR DUTCH OVEN OUTSIDE, TOO

If you have an uncoated cast-iron Dutch oven, you may soon find that cooking over an open fire is a wonderful way to experience new flavors and learn new ways to prepare meals.

As this book focuses solely on in-kitchen use of the Dutch oven, you will not find recipes here for camping. However, I encourage you to experiment with using the Dutch oven for cooking outdoors. Stews, soups, and chilis are great dishes to start with as you try using your Dutch oven under the open sky.

If you plan to use your Dutch oven outdoors, invest in tools for safety. Consider purchasing a camping tripod to suspend the pot above the coals, metal forks to move the lid off the pot, and special high-heat–resistant potholders to protect your hands.

For additional help learning to use your Dutch oven outside, follow the tips from Beyond the Tent (BeyondtheTent.com) or Fresh off the Grid (FreshOfftheGrid.com/camping-recipe-index).

GOLDEN RULES FOR DUTCH OVEN COOKING

Here are a few tips that are sure to make your experience with the Dutch oven successful. These guidelines help make cooking easier and food more delicious while keeping your Dutch oven in good shape for future use.

Don't use high heat when cooking on the stovetop. Because the Dutch oven holds heat so well, it can burn foods easily if the heat is set too high. It is best to cook over medium heat in this pot. Most recipes will indicate that a medium-heat or low-heat setting is best.

Use oven mitts or potholders when handling the lid or handles of the Dutch oven. Unlike some pots and pans with plastic-coated handles, the enamel coating on this pan does not prevent you from being burned. The handles get as hot as the pot you are cooking in, so always keep the oven mitts handy.

Add oil before cooking to prevent any food from sticking. Always bake with a well-greased or oiled Dutch oven to prevent dough or batter from sticking to the pot's interior surface. For cakes, use a coating of butter or shortening and a dusting of flour. When making bread, a coating of oil is ideal. Instructions for cobblers and other desserts vary, and specific directions are noted in each recipe.

Use the lid when you want to retain heat and moisture in any dish. To prevent crusts or tops from browning too fast, leave the lid on for 75 percent of the cooking time. When braising or roasting meats, use the lid to retain moisture. The spikes on the inside of the lid will help with this process even more by returning the moisture to the meat, in effect, basting it while it cooks.

Remove the lid when you want to reduce the liquid in a recipe or sauce. Additionally, when baking bread, remove the lid for the last 25 percent of the cooking time so the edges and top of the loaf brown properly. This can also be a handy trick when roasting skin-on meat that you want to crisp before serving.

Don't overfill the Dutch oven. Never fill the pot more than three-quarters full with batter or dough. As you bake, the dough will expand upward and outward; you do not want your baked goods overflowing the pot and burning. Remember this tip especially when making breads or cakes.

Remove the pot from the oven and let cool for at least 10 minutes before removing biscuits, bread, corn bread, or rolls from the Dutch oven. This helps prevent sticking. For easy removal of breads and biscuits, line the bottom of the Dutch oven with parchment paper.

Remove meats before they reach the desired doneness temperature. Because the Dutch oven holds heat so well, remove meats, such as steaks, at 7° to 10°F lower than the desired doneness temperature. Use a meat thermometer to measure the temperature. Let the meat rest for 10 minutes before serving or cutting it into slices, so it can reach the appropriate temperature.

YOUR COMPLETE DUTCH OVEN KITCHEN

This section explores the items that are great to keep stocked in your pantry, refrigerator, or freezer to create the recipes in this cookbook. Looking beyond these recipes, the lists also include common ingredients that are nice to have on hand to help produce incredible meals in the Dutch oven any time.

Pantry and Counter

Although I keep a plethora of fresh fruits, vegetables, and meats on hand, as well as frozen items for cooking, there are a few staple pantry items that are always beneficial to stock up on. This list includes the items I reach for most often when cooking with my Dutch oven. I recommend keeping a supply of these along with any other ingredients you use regularly.

- Baking powder
- Baking soda
- Beans, canned: cannellini beans, chickpeas, chili beans, great northern beans, kidney beans, and pinto beans
- Beans, dried: black beans, chickpeas, great northern beans, lentils (brown, green, and red), pinto beans, and split peas
- Cocoa powder, unsweetened
- Cornmeal
- Flour, all-purpose
- Oil: nonstick cooking spray, olive oil, and vegetable oil
- Pasta, dried: bow ties, elbow macaroni, lasagna noodles, rotini, spaghetti
- Pecans
- Rice: basmati, brown rice, jasmine rice, and wild rice
- Spices, dried: basil, black pepper, cayenne pepper, chili powder, garlic powder, garlic salt, herbes de Provence, Italian seasoning, minced onion, onion powder, oregano, paprika, rosemary, salt, taco seasoning, and thyme
- Tomatoes, canned: diced tomatoes, tomato paste, and tomato sauce
- Vegetables, canned: carrots, corn, green beans, peas, and mixed vegetables
- Vegetable shortening
- Walnuts
- Yeast, active dry or instant rapid-rise

Refrigerator and Freezer

Great meals also include ingredients found in your refrigerator and freezer. Following you will find some of the staple items I keep on hand for the meals in this book, as well as items that are ideal for helping whip up easy Dutch oven meals on the fly.

- Cheeses: cheddar, cottage, feta, mozzarella, Parmesan, and ricotta
- Dairy: butter, heavy (whipping) cream, Greek yogurt, milk, and sour cream
- Fresh fruits: apples, blackberries, blueberries, lemons, limes, oranges, peaches, and strawberries
- Fresh herbs: basil, cilantro, oregano, rosemary, and thyme
- Fresh or frozen meats: chicken breasts, chicken thighs, chuck roast, ground beef, steaks, and fish

- Fresh produce: asparagus, bell peppers, broccoli, cauliflower, jalapeño peppers, onions, potatoes (white and sweet), and scallions
- Frozen vegetables: broccoli, cauliflower, corn, and peas
- Garlic, minced in oil
- Nondairy milks: almond, coconut, and oat
- Sauces and condiments: barbecue sauce, ketchup, mustard, soy sauce, and Worcestershire sauce

HANDY DUTCH OVEN COMPANIONS

When cooking with a Dutch oven, there are a few other items you'll want to have on hand for safety or convenience. Most Dutch oven recipes will use two to three additional items. Here's what I recommend:

A **blender or immersion blender** for pureeing ingredients or soups.

A quality **chef's knife and paring knife.** These don't have to be expensive, but they do need to be sharp and fit your hand well for safe use.

Cutting boards for meat and fresh produce. Always keep separate cutting boards for use with raw meat, poultry, and seafood as well as a designated board for fresh produce. Plastic boards are best for meats as they are easier to sanitize.

A **handheld mixer or stand mixer** is ideal for mixing batters for cakes or doughs for breads.

Mixing bowls in various sizes for preparing batters and doughs as well as marinating meats.

Oven mitts and potholders to protect your hands from the heat of the pot and lid when moving your Dutch oven from stove to oven, or to the counter for serving.

Silicone tongs are ideal for flipping meat and won't scrape or scratch the bottom of the pot.

Trivets for placing beneath the Dutch oven to protect counters and tables when serving hot out of the oven.

Wooden spoons and spatulas are best for use with an enamel-coated Dutch oven, as they won't scrape or scratch the coating and they are heat resistant.

ABOUT THE RECIPES

While developing the recipes for this book, I used a round enamel-coated Le Creuset 5½-quart Dutch oven. Most recipes were created with the goal of producing 4 to 6 servings.

In choosing which recipes to feature in the cookbook, I opted for a variety of foods that you probably already know and love to introduce you to the joys of using such a versatile cooking vessel. Then, I added unique flavor combinations as well as updates to classics to provide you with a well-rounded collection of both easy and complex dishes that can be made using this amazing kitchen tool.

Note that many recipes call for you to coat your Dutch oven with nonstick cooking spray. Nonstick cooking spray is not included in the recipe ingredient lists, but is a good thing to keep on hand when cooking with the Dutch oven.

Within this cookbook you will find options for breakfast and brunch, home-made breads, side dishes, soups and stews, vegan and vegetarian options, fish and shellfish, poultry, meat, desserts, as well as a selection of staple items such as Couscous (page 155) and Tomato Basil Marinara Sauce (page 159).

Start with something simple like Chicken Bone Broth (page 154), Honey Oat Sandwich Bread (page 40), or Creamy Mashed Potatoes (page 55). Once you are comfortable cooking with the Dutch oven, move on to recipes like Red Lentil Spinach Curry (page 82), Shrimp Scampi (page 106), Prime Rib of Beef (page 134), or decadent Triple Chocolate Cake (page 151).

Recipe Labels

All the recipes in this book include labels to help you select the dishes that are right for you. Recipes with the "Weekend" label require more than 1½ hours of cooking time, and often include more extensive method steps. Recipes labeled "Weeknight" are ready in 45 minutes or less and are practical for preparing after a busy day at work.

Other labels include Dairy-Free, Gluten-Free, Vegetarian, and Vegan, so you can meet the dietary needs of your family and friends. I have used the "One Pot" label to indicate dishes that cook in the Dutch oven from start to finish, with no draining or removing of ingredients and no cooking other components in a different pot.

Recipe Tips

Included with the recipes are tips to guide you through the cooking process, or help you adapt a recipe as needed:

Cooking tip: These tips will help make the cooking process easier, clarify a cooking instruction, or offer suggestions for eliminating messes.

Ingredient tip: These tips navigate sourcing, preparing, or working with an ingredient in the recipe.

Make-ahead tip: If you need help preparing things a bit in advance to make the actual cooking process easier and faster, try these tips. They may include preparing vegetables ahead or making a casserole that is easy to reheat later.

Serving tip: Look here for suggestions for yummy toppings or pairings that will go well with the flavors in the recipe.

Variation tip: For those who like to tinker with flavors, these tips tell you when an ingredient is versatile and can be replaced by a similar item, or offer ideas about how to change the flavors of a recipe and offer advice on changing ingredients to make the recipe suitable for other dietary needs.

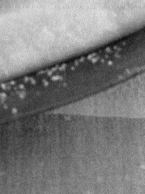

2

BREAKFAST AND BRUNCH

CARROT CAKE BAKED OATMEAL

SERVES 8
PREP TIME: 10 minutes
COOK TIME: 35 minutes
ONE POT, VEGETARIAN

Heart-healthy oats and carrots combine with just enough sweetness to make this breakfast feel decadent while still ensuring a nutritious start to your day. Cooking the oats in the Dutch oven keeps the grains moist for easy slicing.

3 cups rolled oats

1¼ cups grated carrot

¾ cup shredded unsweetened coconut

¼ cup golden raisins

¼ cup chopped pecans

¾ cup packed brown sugar

1¼ teaspoons ground cinnamon

½ teaspoon salt

¼ teaspoon ground nutmeg

¼ teaspoon baking soda

2 large eggs

2½ cups whole milk

½ cup unsweetened applesauce

1 tablespoon vanilla extract

4 tablespoons (½ stick) unsalted butter, melted and cooled

1. Preheat the oven to 350°F. Spray the bottom and sides of a Dutch oven with nonstick cooking spray.

2. In a large bowl, stir together the oats, carrot, coconut, raisins, pecans, brown sugar, cinnamon, salt, nutmeg, and baking soda.

3. In another large bowl, whisk the eggs, milk, applesauce, vanilla, and cooled melted butter until combined. Pour the wet mixture over the dry mixture and stir until combined. Transfer the batter to the prepared Dutch oven.

4. Bake, uncovered, for 35 minutes, or until set and golden on top.

5. Let sit for 10 minutes before cutting into slices and serving hot or cold.

INGREDIENT TIP: To make this dish gluten-free, purchase certified gluten-free oats. Although oats are naturally gluten-free, some are packaged in factories alongside gluten products and can become cross-contaminated.

MAKE-AHEAD TIP: Refrigerate individual portions in airtight containers for 3 to 4 days of on-the-go breakfasts.

BLACK BEAN SALSA CRUSTLESS
QUICHE WITH COTIJA CHEESE

SERVES 6
PREP TIME: 10 minutes
COOK TIME: 45 minutes
GLUTEN-FREE, ONE POT, VEGETARIAN

This quiche brings a classic egg-based breakfast dish to the brunch, lunch, or even dinner table. Inspired by the bright flavors of the Southwestern United States, this dish offers tons of protein and a bit of spice, without bringing too much heat.

8 large eggs
½ cup sour cream
½ cup whole milk
1 teaspoon salt
½ teaspoon freshly ground black pepper
½ teaspoon ground cumin
¼ teaspoon smoked paprika
1 (15-ounce) can black beans, drained and rinsed
2 Roma tomatoes, diced
1 (4-ounce) can diced green chiles
¾ cup crumbled cotija cheese, divided

1. Preheat the oven to 350°F. Spray the bottom and sides of a Dutch oven with nonstick cooking spray.

2. In a large bowl, whisk the eggs, sour cream, milk, salt, pepper, cumin, and paprika until combined. Stir in the black beans, tomatoes, green chiles and ½ cup of cheese. Pour the mixture into the prepared Dutch oven.

3. Bake, uncovered, for 40 to 45 minutes, until the center is set.

4. Sprinkle with the remaining ¼ cup of cheese and serve immediately.

VARIATION TIP: If cotija cheese is not available, substitute shredded cheddar, Colby Jack, or mozzarella cheese.

CARAMEL APPLE
MONKEY BREAD

SERVES 4
PREP TIME: 45 minutes
COOK TIME: 25 minutes
ONE POT, VEGETARIAN

Monkey bread is traditionally prepared in a Bundt-style pan but is well-suited for a Dutch oven variation. This special breakfast treat—with homemade dough and little bits of apple and caramel throughout—is ideal for holidays or weekends with the kids. It can be made ahead and reheated but is best served fresh from the oven with a side of bacon and fresh fruit.

1 cup lukewarm water

⅓ cup vegetable oil

¾ cup sugar, divided

2 tablespoons
  rapid-rise yeast

1 large egg

13 tablespoons unsalted
  butter, melted, divided,
  plus more for greasing

½ teaspoon salt

3 to 3½ cups
  all-purpose flour

2 tablespoons whole milk

1 tablespoon
  ground cinnamon

½ cup chopped apple

½ cup caramel bits or
  caramel pieces, cut into
  pea-size pieces

1. In a large bowl, stir together the warm water, oil, ¼ cup of sugar, and the yeast. Let sit for 5 minutes.

2. Stir in the egg, 1 tablespoon of melted butter, and the salt.

3. Add 3 cups of flour, 1 cup at a time, mixing after each addition, until a dough begins to form. If the dough is still sticky, add the remaining ½ cup of flour, ¼ cup at a time, until the dough is smooth. Set aside for 15 minutes.

4. Position a rack in the middle of the oven and preheat the oven to 350°F. Lightly coat the bottom and sides of a Dutch oven with butter.

5. In a medium bowl, whisk the remaining 12 tablespoons of melted butter, remaining ½ cup of sugar, the milk, and cinnamon to combine, then set aside.

6. Divide the dough into 8 equal parts, then divide each of these parts into 2 pieces, rolling each piece in a ball. Place 8 dough balls into the bottom of the prepared Dutch oven. Top the 8 dough balls with half the butter-sugar mixture, then sprinkle the apple and caramel bits over the top.

7. Place the remaining 8 dough balls over the apple and caramel bits, then drizzle the remaining butter-sugar mixture on top.

8. Cover the pot and bake on the middle rack for 20 to 25 minutes, until golden and the rolls are cooked through. Remove and let cool for 10 minutes before serving.

COOKING TIP: When working with sticky, sugary recipes like this one, line the Dutch oven with aluminum foil to make cleanup easier. This also helps make it easy to pull out the finished dish for serving.

BROWN SUGAR CINNAMON
FRENCH TOAST CASSEROLE

SERVES 6
PREP TIME: 10 minutes
COOK TIME: 30 minutes
ONE POT, VEGETARIAN

French toast is a classic breakfast everyone loves, and this easy version is just as delicious baked as a casserole—perhaps even tastier with extra brown sugar and golden raisins sprinkled in. Serve with syrup, or top with fresh berries and whipped cream for a special treat.

4 tablespoons (½ stick) unsalted butter, melted, plus more for greasing
1½ cups whole milk
6 large eggs
½ cup packed brown sugar, divided
1 tablespoon ground cinnamon
½ teaspoon salt
12 slices cinnamon bread
½ cup golden raisins

1. Preheat the oven to 350°F. Lightly coat the sides and bottom of a Dutch oven with butter.

2. In a large bowl, whisk the milk, eggs, ¼ cup of brown sugar, the cinnamon, and salt to combine.

3. Tear the bread into 1-inch pieces and spread them across the bottom of the prepared Dutch oven.

4. Pour the milk and egg mixture over the bread, making sure to cover all of the bread well. Sprinkle the top with the raisins.

5. In a small bowl, whisk the melted butter and remaining ¼ cup of brown sugar to blend. Drizzle the butter mixture over the bread mixture.

6. Cover the pot and bake for 25 minutes. Remove the lid and bake for 5 minutes more, or until browned.

VARIATION TIP: Replace the golden raisins with chopped pecans, walnuts, or chocolate chips for a variation of texture and flavor.

CHEDDAR AND BACON GRITS

SERVES 4
PREP TIME: 10 minutes
COOK TIME: 35 minutes
GLUTEN-FREE

Grits are a Southern staple, and this recipe is an ideal way to serve them. Their thick, rich texture mixed with the saltiness of bacon and creaminess of cheddar cheese turns something simple into a delicious meal to start your day.

4 bacon slices, chopped
1 shallot, finely diced
1 garlic clove, minced
4½ cups water
1 cup quick-cooking grits
1 cup shredded cheddar
   cheese, divided
¼ teaspoon freshly ground
   black pepper
Salt (optional)
3 scallions, white and
   green parts, diced

1. In a Dutch oven over medium heat, cook the bacon for 5 minutes, or until crisp. Transfer to paper towels to drain, leaving the bacon fat in the pot.

2. Add the shallot and garlic to the bacon fat in the pot and cook for 2 minutes, stirring regularly, until softened.

3. Slowly pour in the water, being careful to avoid being splattered with hot bacon fat. Bring the water to a boil over medium heat. Whisk in the grits. Cook, stirring, until the grits are thickened, then reduce the heat to low and simmer for 20 minutes, stirring every few minutes to prevent sticking.

4. Add ½ cup of cheddar cheese, half the cooked bacon, and the pepper. Stir well until combined and the cheese is melted. Taste and season with salt, if needed.

5. Remove from the heat and serve, topped with the remaining ½ cup of cheese, bacon crumbles, and scallions.

VARIATION TIP: For a boost of flavor, use Chicken Bone Broth (page 154) or Vegetable Broth (page 160), or store-bought broth, in place of water.

COUNTRY SAUSAGE GRAVY

SERVES 6
PREP TIME: 5 minutes
COOK TIME: 15 minutes
ONE POT

Growing up in the South, nothing was more traditional (or delicious) than a plate of biscuits served with classic country sausage gravy. The white gravy is dotted with satisfying bits of breakfast sausage. Creamy, packed with flavor, and ready in minutes, this sausage gravy is the perfect topping for toast or Flaky Buttermilk Biscuits (page 38).

1 pound ground breakfast sausage

1 tablespoon unsalted butter

⅓ cup all-purpose flour

3 cups whole milk

1½ teaspoons freshly ground black pepper

½ teaspoon salt, plus more as needed

¼ teaspoon garlic powder

1. In a Dutch oven over medium heat, crumble and cook the breakfast sausage for 5 to 7 minutes, until cooked through.

2. Add the butter to the sausage and let it melt. Sprinkle the flour over the sausage and stir to coat and combine. While stirring, pour in the milk and cook for 2 to 3 minutes, stirring, until the milk thickens.

3. Stir in the pepper, salt, and garlic powder, then remove from the heat. Taste and add more salt, if needed.

VARIATION TIP: This dish can be made with mild, hot, or maple sausage, or turkey sausage, if needed. When using a leaner sausage, add 2 tablespoons more butter in step 2 to help create the roux.

DUTCH BABY PANCAKE

SERVES 4
PREP TIME: 15 minutes
COOK TIME: 20 minutes
ONE POT, VEGETARIAN

A Dutch baby is a fun twist on the classic breakfast pancake, providing a different style that is baked rather than panfried. This breakfast recipe is a great choice for mornings when you want pancakes but don't want to tend to the stovetop constantly.

3 large eggs
½ cup all-purpose flour
½ cup whole milk
½ teaspoon salt
**2 tablespoons
  unsalted butter**

1. Preheat the oven to 400°F.

2. In a large bowl, beat the eggs until fluffy, then stir in the flour, milk, and salt and mix until smooth.

3. Place the butter in the Dutch oven and place the pot in the oven for 2 to 3 minutes to melt the butter. Remove the Dutch oven from the oven and immediately transfer the batter to the pot.

4. Bake, uncovered, for 20 minutes, or until puffed and golden. Remove and serve.

SERVING TIP: This dish is typically served topped with fresh fruit and whipped cream. You can also serve it with chocolate-hazelnut spread, cream cheese, peanut butter, syrup, or powdered sugar.

FLUFFY CINNAMON ROLLS
WITH CREAM CHEESE FROSTING

SERVES 12
PREP TIME: 30 minutes, plus 1 hour 30 minutes to rise and 15 minutes to cool
COOK TIME: 25 minutes
VEGETARIAN, WEEKEND

A simple yeast dough creates the base for these sweet cinnamon rolls, which are ideal for breakfast and dessert. This is an excellent recipe to make on weekends, as the dough requires some time to rise. It is worth the wait, though, as baking them in the Dutch oven keeps the rolls temptingly moist and soft.

FOR THE DOUGH

2¼ teaspoons active
   dry yeast
¼ cup warm milk
3 tablespoons granulated
   sugar, plus 1 teaspoon
2 cups all-purpose flour,
   plus more for dusting
½ teaspoon salt
6 tablespoons (¾ stick)
   cold unsalted butter
2 large eggs

FOR THE FILLING

⅓ cup packed brown sugar
2½ teaspoons
   ground cinnamon
⅛ teaspoon
   ground nutmeg
8 tablespoons (1 stick)
   unsalted butter, at
   room temperature

1. **To make the dough:** In a small bowl, stir together the yeast, warm milk, and 1 teaspoon of granulated sugar. Set aside for 5 minutes to allow the yeast to bloom.

2. In a large bowl, whisk the flour and salt to combine. Using a fork or pastry blender, cut the cold butter into the flour mixture until the dough is formed into pea-size crumbles.

3. Add the eggs, remaining 3 tablespoons of granulated sugar, and the yeast mixture and stir until a dough forms.

4. Lightly flour a clean work surface and place the dough on it. Knead the dough for 3 minutes. You may need to lightly flour your hands to prevent the dough from sticking.

5. Spray a large bowl with nonstick cooking spray. Place the dough into the prepared bowl, loosely cover with a clean kitchen towel or plastic wrap, and set aside in a warm place for 1 hour, or until the dough doubles in size.

**2 tablespoons
cream cheese, at
room temperature**

2 tablespoons whole milk

**2 tablespoons
powdered sugar**

1 teaspoon vanilla extract

6. **To make the filling:** In a small bowl, stir together the brown sugar, cinnamon, and nutmeg.

7. **To finish the cinnamon rolls:** Once the dough has doubled in size, coat the bottom and sides of a Dutch oven with nonstick cooking spray.

8. Lightly flour a clean work surface and place the dough on it. Roll the dough into a ¼-inch-thick rectangle.

9. Spread the room-temperature butter evenly over the top of the dough and sprinkle the brown sugar mixture evenly over the butter. Starting with the long side closest to you, carefully roll the dough away from you into a log, tucking it in tightly as you roll. Cut the dough into 12 equal pieces and place them, spiral-side up, into the prepared Dutch oven so they are touching on all sides. Loosely cover the Dutch oven with a clean kitchen towel or plastic wrap and set aside for 30 minutes to rise.

10. About 15 minutes into the rising time, preheat the oven to 350°F.

11. Remove the towel and bake the cinnamon rolls, uncovered, for 20 to 25 minutes, until golden brown on top. Remove and set aside for 15 minutes to cool.

CONTINUED

12. **To make the frosting:** In a medium bowl, whisk the cream cheese, milk, powdered sugar, and vanilla until smooth and combined. Spread the frosting over the cooled rolls before serving.

VARIATION TIP: For extra flavor and texture, sprinkle the dough with ¼ cup raisins and ¼ cup chopped pecans after the brown sugar in step 9.

HAM AND POTATO
BREAKFAST HASH

SERVES 6
PREP TIME: 15 minutes
COOK TIME: 20 minutes
GLUTEN-FREE

Sometimes, you just want breakfast that is fast, easy to make, and has everything you crave all in one bite. This hash is just that. Every bite has tender yet crispy bits of potato and ham, plus fresh vegetables and tons of flavor. It's a great way to start your day with taste and nutrition.

1 tablespoon
  unsalted butter

1 tablespoon extra-virgin
  olive oil

1 pound red
  potatoes, cubed

1 teaspoon salt, plus more
  as needed

1 teaspoon freshly ground
  black pepper

1 teaspoon paprika

8 ounces button
  mushrooms, chopped

1 bell pepper, any
  color, chopped

1 small yellow
  onion, chopped

2 garlic cloves, minced

4 ounces ham
  steak, cubed

½ cup shredded cheddar
  cheese (optional)

½ cup salsa (optional)

1. In a Dutch oven over medium heat, melt the butter and heat the oil. Add the potatoes, salt, pepper, and paprika and cook for 5 to 7 minutes, stirring occasionally, until the potatoes begin to brown.

2. Add the mushrooms, bell pepper, onion, and garlic and cook for 5 minutes, stirring regularly, until the vegetables are tender.

3. Stir in the ham and cook for 5 minutes to heat through. Taste and season with additional salt, if needed.

4. Serve topped with the cheddar cheese (if using) or salsa (if using).

VARIATION TIP: Although I prefer using red potatoes, you can also use Yukon Gold potatoes with similar results and cook times. If using russet potatoes, you may need to increase the cook time by 5 minutes.

SPICY TOFU BREAKFAST
BURRITOS

SERVES 6
PREP TIME: 10 minutes
COOK TIME: 10 minutes
VEGAN

Tofu is a perfect substitute for eggs in this easy-to-prepare vegan recipe. Loaded with flavor and with just enough heat, these burritos are an excellent make-ahead meal to have on hand for easy weekday breakfasts.

1½ tablespoons
  extra-virgin olive
  oil, divided
1 garlic clove, minced
1 shallot, minced
½ cup diced
  button mushrooms
½ cup diced green
  bell pepper
1 (14-ounce) package
  firm tofu
1 teaspoon salt
½ teaspoon freshly ground
  black pepper
¼ teaspoon red
  pepper flakes
¼ teaspoon
  cayenne pepper

1. In a Dutch oven over medium heat, heat 1 tablespoon of oil. Add the garlic, shallot, mushrooms, and bell pepper. Cook for 2 minutes, stirring regularly. Transfer the mixture to a bowl and set aside.

2. Pour the remaining ½ tablespoon of oil into the pot and add the tofu. Using a wooden spoon, crumble the tofu. Stir in the salt, black pepper, red pepper flakes, and cayenne. Cook for 1 minute, stirring well, until the tofu is combined with the seasonings.

3. Add the cooked vegetables to the Dutch oven and stir to combine. Cook for 2 minutes.

4. Place the tortillas on a microwave-safe plate and sprinkle with the water. Cover loosely with a paper towel and microwave for 20 to 30 seconds, until heated through.

5. Divide the tofu and vegetables equally among the tortillas and top each with a dash of hot sauce, avocado slices, and vegan cheese (if using).

6 (7- or 8-inch)
  flour tortillas

1 tablespoon water

1 tablespoon hot sauce

1 avocado, peeled, halved,
  pitted, and sliced

Shredded vegan cheese,
  such as Chao, Daiya,
  or Miyoko's, for
  serving (optional)

6. Fold in the left and right sides of the tortillas over the filling. Roll up the burritos from the bottom, making sure to tightly wrap the filling inside. Serve hot.

MAKE-AHEAD TIP: Prepare the tofu scramble as directed, let cool, and refrigerate in an airtight container for up to 5 days. Reheat and assemble the tortillas and toppings when ready to serve.

SPINACH AND MUSHROOM
BREAKFAST CASSEROLE

SERVES 6
PREP TIME: 10 minutes
COOK TIME: 30 minutes
GLUTEN-FREE, VEGETARIAN

Nutritious and delicious, fresh spinach paired with mushrooms creates a surprisingly "meaty" vegetarian dish that works well for a variety of meals. This casserole can be made ahead and reheated to serve later.

2 tablespoons extra-virgin olive oil

8 ounces mushrooms of choice, sliced

1 yellow onion, diced

4 cups fresh baby spinach

8 ounces ricotta cheese

1 cup shredded mozzarella cheese, divided

1 teaspoon garlic powder

½ teaspoon salt

½ teaspoon freshly ground black pepper

⅛ teaspoon red pepper flakes

1. Preheat the oven to 400°F.

2. In a Dutch oven over medium heat, heat the oil. Add the mushrooms and onion and sauté for about 5 minutes or until the mushrooms and onion are soft and beginning to brown. Remove the Dutch oven from the heat.

3. Stir in the spinach, ricotta, ½ cup of mozzarella, the garlic powder, salt, black pepper, and red pepper flakes until combined. Spread the mixture evenly in the pot and top with the remaining ½ cup of mozzarella.

4. Bake, uncovered, for 20 minutes, or until bubbling and the top is golden brown. Serve immediately.

MAKE-AHEAD TIP: Prepare the recipe through step 3 and let cool. Cover and refrigerate until ready to bake. Alternatively, bake the recipe as instructed and let it cool before transferring it to airtight containers. Refrigerate for up to 5 days, or freeze for up to 3 months.

VANILLA BEAN SCONES

SERVES 6
PREP TIME: 10 minutes
COOK TIME: 25 minutes
ONE POT, VEGETARIAN

Light, flaky dough with a rich vanilla bean flavor is a lovely way to start the day. The key to perfect scones is the addition of heavy cream and chilled butter, and this recipe generates beautiful results every time. These scones are delicious served hot with fresh butter or jam.

2 cups all-purpose flour, plus more for dusting

½ cup sugar

2 teaspoons baking powder

½ teaspoon baking soda

½ teaspoon salt

8 tablespoons (1 stick) cold unsalted butter

1 large egg

½ cup heavy (whipping) cream, plus 2 tablespoons

1 tablespoon vanilla bean paste

1. Preheat the oven to 375°F. Line a 5-quart Dutch oven with parchment paper and set aside.

2. In a large bowl, sift together the flour, sugar, baking powder, baking soda, and salt.

3. Grate the cold butter into the dry mixture, then stir until combined.

4. In a small bowl, whisk the egg, ½ cup of heavy cream, and vanilla bean paste until just combined. Pour the cream mixture over the flour mixture and stir until just combined and a sticky dough forms.

5. Lightly dust a clean work surface with flour and place the dough on it. Press the dough into a round about 1½ inches thick. Cut the dough into 6 wedges and place them into the prepared Dutch oven. Brush the scones with the remaining 2 tablespoons of heavy cream.

6. Bake, uncovered, for 25 minutes or until golden. Serve hot.

VARIATION TIP: If you don't have vanilla bean paste, substitute 2 tablespoons vanilla extract.

3

BREAD

QUICK-RISE YEAST
DINNER ROLLS

SERVES 8
PREP TIME: 20 minutes, plus 10 minutes to rise
COOK TIME: 10 minutes
ONE POT, VEGETARIAN, WEEKNIGHT

These fluffy yeast rolls are soft on the inside with a light golden-brown top. They are delicious served alongside Portabella Mushroom Pot Roast (page 86) and are quick enough to whip up for dinner on a busy weeknight.

2 tablespoons unsalted
    butter, at room
    temperature, divided
½ cup warm water
3 tablespoons extra-virgin
    olive oil
2 tablespoons sugar
1 tablespoon active
    dry yeast
¼ teaspoon salt
1 large egg
2½ to 3 cups
    all-purpose flour

1. Preheat the oven to 400°F. Use 1½ teaspoons of butter to coat the bottom and halfway up the sides of a Dutch oven.

2. In a large bowl, stir together the warm water, oil, sugar, yeast, and salt. Set aside for about 5 minutes, or until the yeast is bubbly.

3. Add 1 tablespoon of butter and the egg to the yeast mixture and whisk until combined.

4. Add 2 cups of flour and stir to combine. If the dough is very sticky and still wet, add more flour, ¼ cup at a time, until the dough is soft and no longer sticky.

5. Use the remaining flour to lightly dust a clean work surface and place the dough on it. Knead the dough by hand for 5 to 8 minutes, until smooth and elastic. Loosely cover with a clean kitchen towel or plastic wrap and set aside for 5 to 10 minutes, until the dough just begins to rise.

6. Divide the dough into 8 portions and roll each portion into a ball. Place the dough balls in the prepared Dutch oven in a single layer.

7. In a small microwave-safe dish, melt the remaining 1½ teaspoons of butter and brush it over the rolls.

8. Bake, uncovered, for 10 minutes, or until the rolls have risen and are golden brown on top.

MAKE-AHEAD TIP: This dough can be prepared in advance, divided into balls, and frozen unbaked. When ready to bake, thaw in the refrigerator overnight and let rise in a warm place for 10 minutes before baking as directed.

ARTISAN NO-KNEAD BREAD

SERVES 6
PREP TIME: 15 minutes
COOK TIME: 45 minutes
ONE POT, VEGETARIAN

A dense and somewhat chewy bread, this is a wonderful addition to any meal that suggests serving with a "crusty bread." I love to pair it with Ground Beef Minestrone Soup (page 69). Of course, fresh, warm bread simply served with a bit of butter is excellent as well.

4¼ cups all-purpose flour

1½ teaspoons salt

1½ teaspoons baking soda

4 tablespoons (½ stick)
  unsalted butter, melted

2 teaspoons sugar

2 cups buttermilk, plus
  1 tablespoon

2 tablespoons quick oats

1. Preheat the oven to 400°F. Line a Dutch oven with parchment paper and set aside.

2. In a large bowl, whisk the flour, salt, and baking soda to blend.

3. In a small bowl, stir together the melted butter and sugar. Add the butter mixture to the flour mixture and stir to combine.

4. Gradually add 2 cups of buttermilk to the flour mixture, stirring after each addition, until a dough forms. Transfer the dough to the prepared Dutch oven, brush the top with the remaining 1 tablespoon of buttermilk, and sprinkle with the oats.

5. Slash 2 to 3 lines across the top of the dough about ¼ inch deep.

6. Bake, uncovered, for 45 minutes, or until the dough has risen and is golden brown on top. Remove and let cool for 10 minutes before transferring the loaf from the Dutch oven to serve.

VARIATION TIP: For a different flavor and added texture, sprinkle 1 tablespoon "everything" seasoning over the top of the dough before baking.

CLASSIC CORN BREAD

SERVES 4
PREP TIME: 10 minutes
COOK TIME: 25 minutes
ONE POT, VEGETARIAN, WEEKNIGHT

Slightly sweet, dense, and moist, corn bread is a delicious quick bread that is both classic and comforting. With its hint of corn flavor, it is a perfect companion alongside Pork Stew with Root Vegetables (page 70) or Shredded Beef Chili with Sweet Potatoes (page 72). This recipe is my mom's—I remember enjoying this bread as a child and now serve it to my family, topped with butter and honey.

1½ cups yellow cornmeal

1 teaspoon salt

1 teaspoon baking soda

2 cups buttermilk

3 tablespoons
vegetable oil

1 large egg

1. Preheat the oven to 375°F. Coat a Dutch oven with nonstick cooking spray and set aside.

2. In a large bowl, stir together the cornmeal, salt, and baking soda.

3. Stir in the buttermilk, oil, and egg, stirring until a thick batter forms. Transfer the batter to the prepared Dutch oven.

4. Bake, uncovered, for 20 to 25 minutes, until golden brown.

INGREDIENT TIP: To make this corn bread gluten-free, look for certified gluten-free cornmeal. Cornmeal is naturally gluten-free, but may be produced in facilities that also process wheat products and so can become cross-contaminated.

VARIATION TIP: For a spicy kick, mix in a diced jalapeño pepper. Other variations include adding taco seasoning spices to taste, ½ cup whole kernel corn, or 1 tablespoon honey to the batter.

FLAKY BUTTERMILK BISCUITS

SERVES 6
PREP TIME: 20 minutes
COOK TIME: 15 minutes
ONE POT, VEGETARIAN, WEEKNIGHT

I grew up eating buttermilk biscuits made by my mama and granny, and what follows is my take on their classic recipe. These soft, buttery biscuits are perfect with a bit of butter or with your favorite strawberry jam.

8 tablespoons (1 stick) unsalted butter, diced, plus more for greasing

2½ cups all-purpose flour, plus more for rolling

2 tablespoons baking powder

1 teaspoon salt

1 cup buttermilk

1. Preheat the oven to 400°F. Lightly coat the bottom and sides of a Dutch oven with butter.

2. In a large bowl, stir together the flour, baking powder, and salt until well combined.

3. Using a fork or pastry blender, cut in the cold butter until the dough is formed into pea-size crumbles. Make a well in the center of the dough and pour in the buttermilk. Stir together the flour, butter, and buttermilk until a sticky dough forms.

4. Lightly dust a clean work surface with flour and place the dough in the center, then sprinkle the dough with a bit of flour. Push or roll the dough into a rough square or rectangle, then fold the dough over itself first vertically, then horizontally. Roll this dough until it is ¾ inch thick, then use a round 2- or 3-inch biscuit cutter to cut out 8 to 10 biscuits. Place the biscuits into the prepared Dutch oven with the sides touching.

5. Bake, uncovered, for 15 minutes, or until golden brown on top.

GARLIC PARMESAN
DROP BISCUITS

SERVES 4
PREP TIME: 10 minutes
COOK TIME: 15 minutes
ONE POT, VEGETARIAN, WEEKNIGHT

Flavor-packed garlic Parmesan biscuits pair deliciously with any meal. I love serving these alongside Traditional Chicken Noodle Soup (page 74) or Lemon Pepper Turkey Breast (page 118).

2¼ cups all-purpose flour

2 teaspoons
baking powder

½ teaspoon baking soda

½ teaspoon salt

4 tablespoons
(½ stick) unsalted
butter, diced, plus
1 tablespoon, melted

¼ cup freshly grated
Parmesan cheese

1 teaspoon garlic powder

1 cup buttermilk

1. Preheat the oven to 400°F. Coat a Dutch oven with nonstick cooking spray and set aside.

2. In a large bowl, whisk the flour, baking powder, baking soda, and salt to blend.

3. Using a fork or pastry blender, cut in the diced butter until the dough is formed into pea-size crumbles.

4. Stir in the Parmesan cheese and garlic powder, then gradually stir in the buttermilk, until a sticky dough forms. Drop the dough by spoon-fuls into the prepared Dutch oven, making 8 to 10 biscuits.

5. Bake, uncovered, for 15 minutes, or until golden brown on top. Remove and brush the biscuit tops with the melted butter before serving.

INGREDIENT TIP: No buttermilk? Make your own by putting 1 tablespoon white vinegar into a measuring cup and filling the cup to the 1-cup mark with milk. Let sit for 10 minutes, then use in place of buttermilk in recipes.

HONEY OAT SANDWICH BREAD

SERVES 12
PREP TIME: 20 minutes, plus 1 hour to rise
COOK TIME: 35 minutes
VEGETARIAN, WEEKEND

The light sweetness from the honey in this bread makes it just right for toast and sandwiches. Baking the bread in the Dutch oven allows for even heat distribution, which gives the outside of the bread a nice crust while keeping the inside soft and tender.

3 cups all-purpose
   flour, divided
1 cup rolled oats, plus
   2 tablespoons
2¼ teaspoons active
   dry yeast
1 teaspoon salt
2 tablespoons unsalted
   butter, melted
1 cup evaporated
   milk, warmed
¼ cup honey, plus
   2 tablespoons

1. In a large bowl, whisk 2½ cups of flour, 1 cup of oats, the yeast, and salt until combined.

2. In a medium bowl, whisk the melted butter and evaporated milk to blend. Add ¼ cup of honey and whisk until combined. Add the wet mixture to the dry mixture and mix until a dough forms. If the dough is sticky, add more flour, ¼ cup at a time, until a soft dough forms.

3. Use the remaining flour to lightly dust a clean work surface and place the dough on it. Knead the dough by hand for 5 to 8 minutes, until smooth.

4. Coat another large bowl with nonstick cooking spray. Place the dough ball into the prepared bowl, loosely cover it with a clean kitchen towel or plastic wrap, and set aside in a warm place for 1 hour to rise.

5. Preheat the oven to 350°F. Line a Dutch oven with parchment paper and set aside.

6. Punch down the dough and roll or shape it into a round or log that will fit into your Dutch oven and place the dough into the prepared pot, seam-side down.

7. In a small microwave-safe bowl, microwave the remaining 2 tablespoons of honey for 30 seconds. Brush the top of the dough with the melted honey and sprinkle with the remaining 2 tablespoons of oats.

8. Bake, uncovered, for 30 to 35 minutes, until the dough is risen and golden brown on top.

VARIATION TIP: Whole milk can be used in place of the evaporated milk, if preferred.

PARMESAN PESTO BREAD

SERVES 4
PREP TIME: 20 minutes
COOK TIME: 25 minutes
ONE POT, VEGETARIAN, WEEKNIGHT

Homemade bread in under an hour? It can be done! This recipe is not only a simple homemade bread, but a delicious one loaded with the flavors of pesto and Parmesan. Slice and serve alongside Creamy Red Pepper Chicken Pasta (page 116) or use it as the base for a unique bruschetta at your next party.

2½ cups all-purpose flour, plus more for dusting

½ cup freshly grated Parmesan cheese

2 teaspoons baking powder

½ teaspoon sugar

½ teaspoon salt

¾ cup water

½ cup pesto

2 tablespoons extra-virgin olive oil

1. Preheat the oven to 400°F. Line a Dutch oven with parchment paper and set aside.

2. In a large bowl, whisk the flour, Parmesan cheese, baking powder, sugar, and salt to combine. Pour the water into the flour mixture and mix until just combined and a dough begins to form.

3. Lightly dust a clean work surface with flour. Divide the dough in half and place the halves on the prepared work surface. Flatten each into a square about 1 inch thick. Spread the pesto over one dough square, then top with the remaining square.

4. Gently fold the dough in half two to three times to incorporate the pesto throughout. Place the dough in the prepared Dutch oven and shape into a round loaf. Brush the top of the loaf with the oil.

5. Bake, uncovered, for 25 minutes, or until golden brown on top. Remove and cool the bread for 10 minutes in the Dutch oven before slicing to serve.

ROSEMARY FOCACCIA

Homemade bread is one of my favorite Dutch oven treats, and a delicious focaccia is sure to please. This light, fluffy flatbread is similar in texture to pizza dough, and just as easy to make. Although not a sandwich bread, focaccia is a nice addition to any meal.

1⅓ cups warm water

2 tablespoons
   rapid-rise yeast

2 teaspoons sugar

3½ cups all-purpose flour

¼ cup extra-virgin olive oil,
   plus 1 tablespoon

2 rosemary sprigs, leaves
   removed from the stems

2 teaspoons salt

1. In a large bowl, stir together the warm water, yeast, and sugar. Set aside to proof for 5 minutes.

2. Add the flour, 1 cup at a time, adding the final ½ cup of flour along with ¼ cup of oil, the rosemary, and salt, stirring until a dough forms. Using clean hands, gently knead the dough in the bowl 3 or 4 times, then cover with a damp cloth and let rise for 45 minutes.

3. Preheat the oven to 400°F. Coat the bottom of a Dutch oven with nonstick cooking spray and line it with parchment paper.

4. Place the dough ball into the center of the Dutch oven and shape as desired. Drizzle the loaf with the remaining 1 tablespoon of oil.

5. Bake, uncovered for 30 minutes, or until the dough has risen and is golden brown and cooked through. Remove and let cool in the Dutch oven for 10 minutes before slicing to serve.

VARIATION TIP: Replace the rosemary with any of your favorite fresh herbs, or minced garlic, for a different flavor profile.

SOFT POTATO BREAD

SERVES 6
PREP TIME: 15 minutes, plus 1 hour to rise
COOK TIME: 30 minutes
VEGETARIAN, WEEKEND

Making potato bread is one of my favorite ways to use up leftover potatoes. With only 1 hour of rise time required, this loaf is doable even on a busy weekend, with little hands-on work involved. I like to serve this bread with butter and jam or honey.

1 cup whole milk, warmed

¼ cup warm water

2 tablespoons rapid-rise yeast

4 cups bread flour

1 cup mashed potatoes

4 tablespoons (½ stick) unsalted butter, melted

1 large egg

2 tablespoons sugar

1 teaspoon salt

1. In a large bowl, stir together the milk, warm water, and yeast to combine.

2. Add the flour, mashed potatoes, melted butter, egg, sugar, and salt. Stir until just combined. Using a wooden spoon, fold the dough over itself as if kneading for 3 to 4 minutes. Cover the bowl with a damp kitchen towel and set aside in a warm place for 30 minutes to rise.

3. Coat the bottom and sides of a Dutch oven with nonstick cooking spray.

4. Place the risen dough into the prepared Dutch oven, forming a loaf as desired, then cover the pot with the same damp towel and let rise again for 30 minutes.

5. Preheat the oven to 350°F.

6. Remove the towel and bake the bread, uncovered, for 25 to 30 minutes, until golden brown on top. Transfer to a wire rack to cool completely before slicing to serve.

COOKING TIP: This bread is very light and does not slice well when warm. For best results, let cool completely before slicing.

INGREDIENT TIP: If you do not have mashed potatoes already made, substitute equal amounts of prepared instant mashed potatoes in this recipe.

BRIOCHE LOAF

SERVES 6

PREP TIME: 15 minutes, plus 30 minutes to rest, 10 minutes to knead, and 15 minutes to rise

COOK TIME: 30 minutes

VEGETARIAN, WEEKEND

Soft and airy in texture, brioche is a buttery bread that is slightly sweet and often used as a dessert bread, though it can easily complement your favorite savory dish. I love pairing this brioche with my braised Barbecue Pulled Pork (page 124).

1 cup whole milk

3 cups all-purpose flour, divided

½ cup sugar

2 tablespoons rapid-rise yeast

3 large eggs plus 1 large egg white

2 teaspoons vanilla extract

12 tablespoons (1½ sticks) unsalted butter, melted and cooled

1 tablespoon water

1. In a large bowl, whisk the milk, 1 cup of flour, the sugar, and yeast to combine. Cover the bowl with a clean kitchen towel or plastic wrap and set aside for 30 minutes to rest.

2. Line a Dutch oven with parchment paper.

3. In another large bowl, whisk the whole eggs and vanilla to blend. Add the cooled melted butter and whisk to combine. Add the egg mixture to the yeast mixture and stir well. Gradually stir in the remaining 2 cups of flour until a dough forms. Using a wooden spoon, continuing stirring and folding the dough for about 10 minutes until it becomes elastic and smooth.

4. Preheat the oven to 350°F.

5. In a small bowl, whisk the egg white and water to create a wash.

6. Place the dough into the prepared Dutch oven and brush the top with the egg wash. Let rise for 15 minutes.

7. Bake, uncovered, for 30 minutes, or until golden brown. Transfer the brioche to a wire rack to cool for 15 minutes before slicing to serve.

COOKING TIP: Depending on the type of flour used and the humidity where you are located, you may need to use up to ½ cup more flour to reach the smooth elasticity desired.

4

SIDES

BACON-FRIED
BRUSSELS SPROUTS

SERVES 4
PREP TIME: 10 minutes
COOK TIME: 20 minutes
DAIRY-FREE, GLUTEN-FREE, ONE POT, WEEKNIGHT

Brussels sprouts aren't scary—not even for the pickiest eaters—when you add bacon, shallots, and garlic. Sliced thin and quickly cooked, these Brussels sprouts offer a crisp texture that eats like a snack and is loaded with salty crunch in every bite.

8 ounces bacon, diced
1 pound Brussels sprouts, quartered
1 shallot, minced
2 garlic cloves, minced
½ teaspoon freshly ground black pepper
Salt

1. In a Dutch oven over medium heat, cook the bacon for 5 minutes until crisp. Transfer the bacon to paper towels to drain, leaving the bacon fat in the pot.

2. Add the Brussels sprouts, shallot, and garlic to the bacon fat in the pot and cook for 5 minutes, stirring regularly, until lightly browned.

3. Reduce the heat to low, add the pepper and cooked bacon, and cook for 10 minutes, stirring regularly, until the Brussels sprouts reach your desired tenderness.

4. Taste and season with salt before serving.

SERVING TIP: If your diet allows, top these sprouts with shredded sharp cheddar cheese just before serving to add creaminess to the dish.

MOLASSES BAKED BEANS

SERVES 6
PREP TIME: 15 minutes
COOK TIME: 1 hour
DAIRY-FREE, ONE POT

These sweet and spicy beans are packed with bits of bacon, chopped bell pepper, onion, and fragrant garlic. The beans take about 45 minutes in the oven, but that molasses and vinegar flavor is worth the wait.

8 ounces bacon, diced

1 small yellow onion, diced

½ green bell pepper, diced

3 garlic cloves, minced

1 (15-ounce) can light
   kidney beans, drained
   and rinsed

1 (15-ounce) can pinto
   beans, drained
   and rinsed

1 (15-ounce) can great
   northern beans, drained
   and rinsed

1 cup ketchup

½ cup packed brown sugar

¼ cup yellow mustard

¼ cup apple cider vinegar

2 tablespoons
   dark molasses

1 tablespoon
   Worcestershire sauce

1 teaspoon
   smoked paprika

½ teaspoon chili powder

½ teaspoon salt

1. Preheat the oven to 400°F.

2. In a Dutch oven over medium heat, cook the bacon for 5 minutes until crisp. Transfer to paper towels to drain, leaving the bacon fat in the pot.

3. Add the onion, bell pepper, and garlic to the bacon fat in the pot and cook for 3 to 4 minutes, until the vegetables begin to soften.

4. Add the kidney beans, pinto beans, and great northern beans. Stir in the ketchup, brown sugar, mustard, vinegar, molasses, Worcestershire sauce, paprika, chili powder, salt, and half of the cooked bacon. Spread out the beans evenly.

5. Cover the pot and bake for 30 minutes. Remove the lid and bake for 15 minutes, or until thickened. Serve the beans with the remaining crumbled bacon on top.

VARIATION TIP: Use 3 (15-ounce) cans of the same beans in place of the three-bean mixture, if preferred.

BROWN SUGAR AND
SAGE BLACK-EYED PEAS

SERVES 4
PREP TIME: 10 minutes
COOK TIME: 30 minutes
DAIRY-FREE, GLUTEN-FREE, ONE POT, WEEKNIGHT

Black-eyed peas come to life with this unique seasoning blend of sage and brown sugar. A slightly sweet but rich combination of flavors creates the perfect umami taste in every bite.

8 ounces bacon, diced

½ yellow onion, diced

2 garlic cloves, minced

1 (10-ounce) package frozen black-eyed peas

2 tablespoons packed brown sugar

1 teaspoon dried sage

½ teaspoon freshly ground black pepper

Salt

3 scallions, white and green parts, chopped

1. In a Dutch oven over medium heat, cook the bacon for 5 minutes until crisp. Transfer to paper towels to drain, leaving the bacon fat in the pot.

2. Add the onion and garlic to the bacon fat in the pot and cook for 2 to 3 minutes, stirring regularly, until softened.

3. Stir in the black-eyed peas, brown sugar, sage, and pepper to combine. Reduce the heat to low and simmer for 15 minutes to heat through.

4. Stir in the bacon and cook for 2 to 3 minutes, stirring, until the bacon is heated through. Taste and season with salt.

5. Serve topped with the scallions.

INGREDIENT TIP: If using canned black-eyed peas, drain and rinse them before adding to the Dutch oven.

SCALLOPED POTATOES

SERVES 6
PREP TIME: 15 minutes
COOK TIME: 1 hour
ONE POT, VEGETARIAN

As in a classic scalloped potatoes recipe, these are not loaded with cheese, but rather have a rich and thick, creamy sauce that is ideal for creating tender potatoes when baked.

6 tablespoons (¾ stick) unsalted butter

1 medium yellow onion, thinly sliced

2 garlic cloves, minced

¼ cup all-purpose flour

1 teaspoon dried rosemary

1 teaspoon salt

1 teaspoon freshly ground black pepper

2 cups whole milk

1 cup Vegetable Broth (page 160) or store-bought

3 pounds Yukon Gold potatoes, peeled and cut into ¼-inch-thick slices

2 tablespoons chopped fresh parsley (optional)

1. Preheat the oven to 375°F.

2. In a Dutch oven over medium heat, melt the butter. Add the onion and garlic and cook for 5 minutes, or until the onion is softened.

3. Stir in the flour, rosemary, salt, and pepper to coat the vegetables.

4. Slowly stir in the milk until combined. Add the broth, reduce the heat to low, and simmer for 5 minutes, stirring occasionally, until thickened.

5. Remove from the heat and add the potatoes, making sure they are submerged and coated well with the sauce.

6. Cover the pot and bake for 30 minutes. Remove the lid and bake for 15 minutes, or until the top is browned. Serve topped with the parsley (if using).

COOKING TIP: If you prefer the layered look of the traditional scalloped potato dish, pour the sauce out of the Dutch oven once cooked, then layer the potato slices in the pot before baking. To layer, place one-third of the potatoes in the Dutch oven and top with one-third of the sauce. Repeat with the remaining potatoes and sauce, ending with sauce. Bake as directed.

CREAMED SWEET CORN

SERVES 4
PREP TIME: 10 minutes
COOK TIME: 25 minutes
ONE POT, VEGETARIAN, WEEKNIGHT

This creamed corn dish is a great side for meals year-round. Sweet corn pairs beautifully with the saltiness of Parmesan cheese and just enough dried herbs to elevate the overall flavors. This corn is anything but "plain" and is a great choice for your next weekend barbecue or holiday meal.

4 tablespoons (½ stick)
   unsalted butter

1 small yellow onion, diced

2 garlic cloves, minced

2 tablespoons
   all-purpose flour

1½ cups whole milk

½ cup heavy
   (whipping) cream

4 cups whole kernel corn

¼ cup freshly grated
   Parmesan cheese

1 tablespoon sugar

1 teaspoon salt, plus more
   as needed

½ teaspoon freshly ground
   black pepper, plus more
   as needed

½ teaspoon dried thyme

1. In a Dutch oven over medium heat, melt the butter. Add the onion and garlic and cook for 3 to 4 minutes, stirring regularly, until tender.

2. Stir in the flour to coat the onion and garlic. Stir in the milk and heavy cream.

3. Add the corn, Parmesan, sugar, salt, pepper, and thyme and stir well to combine, then reduce the heat to low. Simmer for 15 minutes, stirring occasionally, until thickened. Taste and season with additional salt and pepper, as needed.

VARIATION TIP: For a brighter flavor, add ½ red bell pepper, diced, to the onion and garlic in step 1.

CREAMY MASHED POTATOES

SERVES 6
PREP TIME: 10 minutes
COOK TIME: 25 minutes
GLUTEN-FREE, VEGETARIAN, WEEKNIGHT

There is no potato dish more classic than creamy mashed potatoes. This simple recipe combines old-school technique with the richness of cream to create a decadent dish that is anything but ordinary.

2 pounds Yukon Gold potatoes, peeled and cubed

1½ teaspoons salt, divided

4 tablespoons (½ stick) unsalted butter

½ cup heavy (whipping) cream

½ cup sour cream

½ teaspoon freshly ground black pepper

¼ teaspoon dried chives

⅛ teaspoon ground sage

Melted unsalted butter, for serving (optional)

1. In a Dutch oven, combine the potatoes with enough water to cover by at least 1 inch. Add 1 teaspoon of salt to the water. Place the pot over medium-high heat and bring the water to a boil. Reduce the heat to medium and cook for 12 to 15 minutes, until the potatoes are fork-tender. Drain the potatoes and return them to the Dutch oven.

2. Place the pot over low heat and add the butter to the potatoes. Gently mash until the butter has melted.

3. Add the heavy cream, sour cream, pepper, chives, and sage. Using a handheld mixer, mix for 2 minutes on medium speed until creamy, being careful not to overmix the potatoes or they will be gummy. Taste and season with the remaining ½ teaspoon of salt, as needed.

4. Serve with additional melted butter drizzled over the top (if using).

COOKING TIP: If you prefer a chunky mashed potato, hand mashing with a wooden spoon or potato masher is all that is needed in step 3.

LEMON-GARLIC GREEN BEANS

SERVES 4
PREP TIME: 10 minutes
COOK TIME: 15 minutes
GLUTEN-FREE, VEGETARIAN, WEEKNIGHT

Fast and fresh dishes are a must in my house, and this recipe for lemon-garlic green beans takes an ordinary vegetable and turns it into a delicious side packed with flavor. The richness of the garlic is offset by bright lemon zest to create a fresh spin on a classic dish.

1 pound green beans,
  trimmed
½ cup water
2 tablespoons
  unsalted butter
1 tablespoon extra-virgin
  olive oil
2 garlic cloves, minced
Grated zest of 1 lemon
½ teaspoon salt
¼ teaspoon freshly ground
  black pepper
Pinch red pepper flakes

1. In a Dutch oven over medium heat, combine the green beans and water and bring the water to a boil. Cook for 3 minutes, or until just tender. Drain the green beans and set aside.

2. Return the Dutch oven to medium heat and place the butter in the pot to melt and pour in the oil to heat. Add the garlic and cook for 1 minute, or until golden.

3. Add the green beans, lemon zest, salt, and black pepper. Cook for 5 minutes, stirring occasionally, until the bean reach your desired tenderness.

4. Stir in the red pepper flakes before serving.

COOKING TIP: If you prefer more tender green beans, boil or steam the beans longer to soften them to your liking.

INGREDIENT TIP: If using canned green beans instead of fresh, skip step 1.

SAUTÉED GARLIC KALE

WITH RED PEPPERS

SERVES 4
PREP TIME: 15 minutes
COOK TIME: 15 minutes
GLUTEN-FREE, ONE POT, VEGAN, WEEKNIGHT

A bit of garlic and just a hint of lemon turn cooked kale into a delicious side dish packed with nutrients. This kale is great with nearly any meal, but pairs especially well with Coconut Curry Braised Chicken Thighs (page 117).

1 tablespoon extra-virgin
olive oil

2 bunches kale, stemmed
and leaves torn
into pieces

1 red bell pepper, diced

2 garlic cloves, minced

¼ cup Vegetable
Broth (page 160)
or store-bought

1 teaspoon freshly
squeezed lemon juice

½ teaspoon salt, plus
more as needed

½ teaspoon freshly ground
black pepper

1. In a Dutch oven over medium heat, heat the oil. Add the kale, bell pepper, and garlic. Sauté for 3 minutes, stirring occasionally, until heated through. Stir in the broth, lemon juice, salt, and pepper.

2. Cover the pot and cook for 10 minutes, or until the vegetables are tender and the broth is reduced.

3. Taste and season with additional salt, if needed, before serving.

INGREDIENT TIP: If you find kale tough or bitter, gently massage the kale leaves with a small amount of oil before cooking, which helps break down the leaves for better texture and flavor.

SOUTHERN CORN BREAD
DRESSING

SERVES 8
PREP TIME: 20 minutes
COOK TIME: 1 hour 10 minutes
WEEKEND

In my house, the holidays just aren't complete without this richly seasoned corn bread stuffing. It has tons of flavor and generous chunks of chicken and is ideal for a meal in itself or as a side at your next holiday gathering.

4 tablespoons (½ stick) unsalted butter

2 tablespoons extra-virgin olive oil

1 pound boneless, skinless chicken breasts, cubed

1 large white onion, chopped

3 celery stalks, chopped

¼ cup all-purpose flour

Classic Corn Bread (page 37)

1 teaspoon dried sage

1 teaspoon dried thyme

1 teaspoon garlic powder

1 teaspoon onion powder

1 teaspoon freshly ground black pepper

½ teaspoon salt

5 cups Chicken Bone Broth (page 154) or store-bought

2 large eggs

1. Preheat the oven to 350°F.

2. In a Dutch oven over medium heat, melt the butter and heat the oil. Add the chicken and cook for 3 minutes, stirring regularly, until browned. Add the onion and celery and cook for 5 minutes, or until softened.

3. Stir in the flour to coat the vegetables and chicken.

4. Remove the mixture from the heat and crumble in the corn bread, sage, thyme, garlic powder, onion powder, pepper, and salt.

5. Stir in the broth and eggs, stirring until all the bread is moistened. Smooth the top into an even layer.

6. Bake, uncovered, for 1 hour, or until a toothpick inserted in the center comes out clean.

7. Slice and serve.

INGREDIENT TIP: If available, fresh sage and fresh thyme are ideal for this recipe. Use 1½ times the amount of fresh as you would dried.

WHOLE ROASTED

CAULIFLOWER

SERVES 6
PREP TIME: 15 minutes
COOK TIME: 1 hour 30 minutes
GLUTEN-FREE, VEGETARIAN, WEEKEND

This preparation ensures you'll never look at cauliflower the same way again. Roasting the whole cauliflower head imparts delicious flavor and creates a richness you won't find with any other cooking method. Lightly spiced and fork-tender, this cauliflower is a perfect choice to serve alongside any of your favorite proteins.

¼ cup extra-virgin olive oil

2 garlic cloves, crushed

1 teaspoon dried oregano

½ teaspoon
  smoked paprika

½ teaspoon salt

1 whole head
  cauliflower, cored

4 tablespoons garlic
  butter (optional)

1. Preheat the oven to 425°F.

2. In a small bowl, whisk the oil, garlic, oregano, paprika, and salt to blend.

3. Place the cauliflower in a Dutch oven and drizzle it with the seasoned oil mixture. Brush the oil all over the cauliflower to coat it well.

4. Cover the pot and bake for 30 minutes, or until heated through. Remove the lid and bake for 1 hour, or until the cauliflower is fork-tender and browned.

5. Serve with garlic butter (if using) for brushing and dipping.

COOKING TIP: For a large head of cauliflower, you may need to add 15 to 20 minutes to the cook time. To determine if the cauliflower is cooked through, use a skewer to pierce the cauliflower through a piece of stem. If the skewer slides in easily, the cauliflower is done.

5

CHAPTER FIVE

SOUPS AND STEWS

BROCCOLI CHEDDAR SOUP

SERVES 6
PREP TIME: 10 minutes
COOK TIME: 35 minutes
ONE POT, VEGETARIAN, WEEKNIGHT

Broccoli cheddar soup is a perfect weeknight comfort food, and this recipe kicks it up a notch with added vegetables. Compared to some classic versions of this cheesy soup, this recipe requires less cream, providing a lighter option for a weeknight family meal.

2 tablespoons
  unsalted butter
2 cups chopped broccoli
1 large potato, peeled
  and chopped
1 carrot, chopped
3 garlic cloves, minced
¼ cup all-purpose flour
4 cups Vegetable
  Broth (page 160)
  or store-bought
2 cups half-and-half
4 ounces cream cheese,
  at room temperature
1 teaspoon
  smoked paprika
1 teaspoon freshly ground
  black pepper
½ cup shredded sharp
  cheddar cheese
Salt
3 scallions, white and
  green parts, chopped

1. In a Dutch oven over medium heat, melt the butter. Add the broccoli, potato, carrot, and garlic. Cook for 5 minutes, stirring regularly, until the vegetables begin to brown.

2. Stir in the flour, coating the vegetables, then add the broth and cook for 10 minutes, or until the vegetables are fork-tender.

3. Reduce the heat to low and stir in the half-and-half, cream cheese, paprika, and pepper.

4. Gradually stir in the cheddar cheese and cook, stirring, for 3 to 5 minutes, until melted. Taste and season with salt, as needed.

5. Reduce the heat to low and simmer for 10 minutes to thicken the soup slightly. Serve topped with the scallions.

INGREDIENT TIP: Although pre-shredded cheese is convenient, for this recipe, it is important to shred your own cheese. It melts better and provides a richer flavor in the soup.

BUTTERNUT SQUASH
GINGER SOUP

SERVES 6
PREP TIME: 20 minutes
COOK TIME: 40 minutes
GLUTEN-FREE, ONE POT, VEGAN

Squash is a wonderful option to create a thick and creamy soup without dairy. The addition of ginger and turmeric warms the sweetness of the squash, creating a cozy cool-weather meal.

2 tablespoons extra-virgin olive oil

1 yellow onion, diced

1 tablespoon grated peeled fresh ginger

3 garlic cloves, minced

4 cups cubed butternut squash

4 cups Vegetable Broth (page 160) or store-bought

1 (15-ounce) full-fat coconut milk

1½ teaspoons ground turmeric

1 teaspoon salt, plus more as needed

½ teaspoon freshly ground black pepper

2 tablespoons chopped fresh cilantro

1. In a Dutch oven over medium heat, heat the oil. Add the onion and cook for 5 minutes, stirring regularly.

2. Add the ginger and garlic and cook for 1 minute, stirring regularly. Add the squash, broth, coconut milk, turmeric, salt, and pepper. Bring the soup to a boil.

3. Reduce the heat to medium-low and simmer, uncovered, for 25 minutes.

4. Using an immersion blender, or in a traditional blender, puree the soup until smooth.

5. Taste and season with more salt, as needed. Serve topped with the cilantro.

INGREDIENT TIP: To save time, use frozen butternut squash cubes in place of fresh squash.

CHICKEN AND HOMEMADE
DUMPLINGS

SERVES 6
PREP TIME: 15 minutes
COOK TIME: 40 minutes
DAIRY-FREE, ONE POT

This classic Southern staple was a common meal in my home when I was growing up. Although my mom often used a baking mix for the dumplings out of convenience, it was the rich, thick broth and extra black pepper that made her version of chicken and dumplings the best. In this version, you'll enjoy my mom's delicious chicken broth plus fresh, handmade dumplings.

FOR THE CHICKEN

1 pound boneless, skinless chicken breasts, cut into 1-inch chunks

1 teaspoon salt

1 teaspoon freshly ground black pepper

2 tablespoons vegetable oil

3 garlic cloves, minced

¼ cup all-purpose flour

4 cups Chicken Bone Broth (page 154) or store-bought

1. **To make the chicken:** Season the chicken all over with the salt and pepper.

2. In a Dutch oven over medium heat, heat the oil. Add the chicken and garlic and cook for 5 minutes, stirring regularly, to brown all sides. Stir in the flour to coat the chicken. Pour in the broth and bring the mixture to a boil.

3. Cover the pot and cook for 20 minutes over medium heat until the chicken is cooked through and the sauce is thickened.

4. **To make the dumplings:** In a medium bowl, stir together the flour, broth, baking powder, salt, and pepper until combined and a loose dough forms.

5. Remove the lid from the Dutch oven and drop the dumpling dough into the boiling broth mixture by the tablespoon. Stir the mixture, reduce the heat to low, and cook for 10 minutes, uncovered, until the dumplings float and are cooked through.

FOR THE DUMPLINGS

2 cups all-purpose flour

**1⅓ cups Chicken Bone
    Broth (page 154)
    or store-bought**

**1 tablespoon
    baking powder**

½ teaspoon salt

**½ teaspoon freshly ground
    black pepper, plus more
    as needed**

**2 tablespoons chopped
    fresh parsley (optional)**

6. Taste and season with more pepper, as needed,
    and top with parsley (if using).

VARIATION TIP: Some people enjoy adding carrots,
onions, celery, or peas to their chicken and dumplings. Although I like to serve these vegetables on the
side, you can add them to the broth to cook before
adding the dumplings.

CHUNKY VEGETABLE SOUP

SERVES 4
PREP TIME: 15 minutes
COOK TIME: 35 minutes
GLUTEN-FREE, ONE POT, VEGAN

This simple vegetable soup is inspired by one I grew up on. Although that soup usually only had carrots and potatoes, I like adding more vegetables for nutrition and flavor. The robust combination of ingredients creates a delicious broth that needs little seasoning and goes great with Classic Corn Bread (page 37).

1 tablespoon extra-virgin
   olive oil
1 yellow onion, diced
2 celery stalks, diced
2 garlic cloves, minced
4 cups Vegetable Broth
   (page 160), store-bought,
   or water
2 large potatoes, peeled
   and cubed
2 carrots, diced
1 (14.5-ounce) can
   diced tomatoes
1 cup diced broccoli
1 cup diced cauliflower
2 tablespoons
   tomato paste
1 teaspoon celery salt
1 teaspoon freshly ground
   black pepper
½ teaspoon dried thyme
Salt

1. In a Dutch oven over medium heat, heat the oil. Add the onion, celery, and garlic and cook for 5 minutes, stirring occasionally, until softened.

2. Add the broth, potatoes, carrots, tomatoes and their juices, broccoli, cauliflower, tomato paste, celery salt, pepper, and thyme. Bring the soup to a simmer and cook for 25 minutes, stirring regularly, until the vegetables are fork-tender.

3. Taste and season with salt, as needed.

VARIATION TIP: This recipe can be personalized by adding different vegetables. Zucchini, yellow squash, okra, and green beans are all delicious when added to the mix.

CREAMY CORN CHOWDER

SERVES 4
PREP TIME: 15 minutes
COOK TIME: 40 minutes
GLUTEN-FREE, ONE POT

This corn chowder is loaded with flavor, and it makes an ideal meal when you have little time and are low on ingredients. I love that this soup is an easy pantry meal that tastes like you worked for hours over a stove.

- 1 tablespoon extra-virgin olive oil
- 1 white onion, diced
- 1 jalapeño pepper, seeded and diced
- 4 garlic cloves, minced
- 3 cups Vegetable Broth (page 160) or store-bought
- 3 cups whole kernel corn (fresh or frozen)
- 1 large potato, peeled and cubed
- 1 teaspoon dried thyme
- 1 teaspoon smoked paprika
- 1 teaspoon freshly ground black pepper
- 1 teaspoon salt
- 1 cup heavy (whipping) cream
- 2 bacon slices, cooked and crumbled (optional)
- ½ cup shredded cheddar cheese (optional)
- 2 scallions, chopped (optional)

1. In a Dutch oven over medium heat, heat the oil. Add the onion, jalapeño, and garlic and cook for 5 minutes, stirring regularly, until softened.

2. Add the broth, corn, potato, thyme, paprika, pepper, and salt. Bring the soup to a simmer and cook for 20 minutes, or until the potatoes are tender.

3. Stir in the cream and cook for 10 minutes to heat through.

4. If desired, served topped with bacon, cheddar, and/or scallions.

MAKE-AHEAD TIP: Let the soup cool completely before portioning it into airtight containers, labeling the containers with the date and recipe name, then freezing for up to 4 months. When freezing, make sure to leave 1 inch of headspace at the top of the container for expansion.

CURRIED CHICKEN STEW

SERVES 4
PREP TIME: 10 minutes
COOK TIME: 1 hour
DAIRY-FREE, GLUTEN-FREE, ONE POT

One evening, when making a favorite easy curry, my sauce didn't quite thicken up as expected and was almost soupy in consistency. That result was the inspiration for this stew, which is packed with protein and warm curry flavor. This stew is best served with fresh naan bread.

1 pound boneless, skinless
  chicken breasts, cut into
  1-inch pieces
4 cups Chicken Bone
  Broth (page 154)
  or store-bought
2 cups full-fat
  coconut milk
1 potato, peeled and cubed
1 (15-ounce) can chick-
  peas, drained and rinsed
½ green bell
  pepper, chopped
4 garlic cloves, minced
1 tablespoon curry powder
1 teaspoon
  ground turmeric
1 teaspoon freshly ground
  black pepper
½ teaspoon
  smoked paprika
Salt

1. In a Dutch oven over medium heat, combine the chicken, broth, coconut milk, potato, chickpeas, bell pepper, garlic, curry powder, turmeric, black pepper, and paprika. Stir to combine. Bring to a boil, then reduce the heat to low and simmer the soup for 45 minutes, stirring occasionally, to meld the flavors.

2. Taste and season with salt, as needed.

VARIATION TIP: Use chicken thighs in place of chicken breasts for a slightly richer flavor. Trim any excess fat from the thighs and cube the meat as you would the breasts.

GROUND BEEF

MINESTRONE SOUP

SERVES 6
PREP TIME: 15 minutes
COOK TIME: 30 minutes
DAIRY-FREE, ONE POT, WEEKNIGHT

This minestrone is the perfect fast meal that has a little of everything in each bowl. Taking inspiration from the traditional Italian soup, I add ground beef for extra flavor and nutrition. What appears to be a random mixture of ingredients emerges as a delicious bowl including meat, vegetables, broth, and pasta.

1 tablespoon extra-virgin olive oil

1 pound ground beef

1 small yellow onion, diced

2 celery stalks, chopped

2 garlic cloves, minced

4 cups beef broth

1 (15-ounce) can light red kidney beans, drained and rinsed

1 (14.5-ounce) can diced tomatoes

1 (10-ounce) package frozen mixed vegetables

2 tablespoons tomato paste

1 teaspoon dried basil

1 teaspoon dried thyme

1 teaspoon dried oregano

1 bay leaf

4 ounces elbow macaroni

Salt

1. In a Dutch oven over medium heat, heat the oil. Add the ground beef, onion, celery, and garlic and cook for 5 to 7 minutes, until the beef is cooked through.

2. Add the broth, kidney beans, tomatoes and their juices, mixed vegetables, tomato paste, basil, thyme, oregano, and bay leaf. Bring the soup to a boil over medium heat and cook for 10 minutes to meld the flavors.

3. Add the macaroni and cook for 8 minutes, or until the pasta is al dente.

4. Taste and season with salt, as needed.

VARIATION TIP: Use ground turkey or ground chicken in place of the ground beef in this recipe, if preferred. Additionally, any small pasta works well in this soup.

PORK STEW WITH
ROOT VEGETABLES

SERVES 4
PREP TIME: 20 minutes
COOK TIME: 1 hour 10 minutes
DAIRY-FREE, WEEKEND

This pork stew is a perfect combination of broth, tender chunks of pork, and a variety of fresh vegetables. Using seasoned salt adds a unique richness to the broth that really complements the pork. Serve the stew with crusty bread on the side.

2 tablespoons
all-purpose flour

½ teaspoon seasoned salt

1 pound boneless
pork roast, cut into
1-inch chunks

2 tablespoons
vegetable oil

1 small yellow
onion, chopped

2 garlic cloves, minced

4 cups Chicken Bone
Broth (page 154)
or store-bought

1 (14.5-ounce) can
diced tomatoes

1 large potato, peeled and
cut into ½-inch pieces

1 celery stalk, cut into
½-inch pieces

1 carrot, cut into
½-inch pieces

1. In a medium bowl, whisk the flour and seasoned salt to blend. Dredge the pork cubes in the seasoned flour, lightly coating them on all sides.

2. In a Dutch oven over medium heat, heat the oil. Add the seasoned pork and cook for 2 to 3 minutes on all sides to add a nice sear. Remove and set aside.

3. In the Dutch oven, combine the onion and garlic and cook for about 2 minutes, or until the onion softens and the garlic is fragrant, scraping any browned bits left from the pork from the bottom of the pot with a wooden spoon.

4. Pour in the broth and the tomatoes and their juices. Add the potato, celery, carrot, Worcestershire sauce, bay leaf, thyme, and oregano. Stir to combine.

5. Return the pork to the pot and bring the mixture to a boil over medium heat. Reduce the heat to low.

1 tablespoon
  Worcestershire sauce
1 bay leaf
½ teaspoon dried thyme
½ teaspoon dried oregano
2 tablespoons chopped
  fresh parsley (optional)

6. Cover the pot and simmer for 45 minutes, or until the pork is cooked through and tender. Serve topped with the parsley (if using).

VARIATION TIP: If your family enjoys mushrooms, add some chopped baby bella mushrooms with the onion and garlic, sauté, then continue cooking as directed.

SHREDDED BEEF CHILI
WITH SWEET POTATOES

SERVES 6
PREP TIME: 15 minutes
COOK TIME: 4 hours 45 minutes
DAIRY-FREE, GLUTEN-FREE, WEEKEND

Slowly cooking this chili allows a tough cut of beef to tenderize and the herbs and spices to meld for a meal that is satisfying and comforting.

2 pounds chuck roast

2 tablespoons
vegetable oil

1 red onion, diced

3 garlic cloves, minced

4 cups beef broth

2 (15-ounce) cans kidney
beans, drained

1 (28-ounce) can
diced tomatoes

1 (28-ounce) can
tomato sauce

1 (6-ounce) can
tomato paste

1 (4-ounce) can diced
green chiles

1 tablespoon ground cumin

2 teaspoons
smoked paprika

2 teaspoons chili powder

1 teaspoon salt

1 teaspoon freshly ground
black pepper

½ teaspoon dried oregano

2 medium sweet potatoes,
peeled and cubed

1. Trim any excess fat off the chuck roast and cut the roast into 8 pieces.

2. In a Dutch oven over medium heat, heat the oil. Add the beef pieces and sear for 2 to 3 minutes on all sides. Transfer the beef to a plate and set aside.

3. In the Dutch oven, combine the red onion and garlic and sauté for 5 minutes, or until softened.

4. Add the broth, kidney beans, tomatoes and their juices, tomato sauce, tomato paste, green chiles and their juices, cumin, paprika, chili powder, salt, pepper, and oregano. Stir to combine and return the beef to the pot.

5. Cover the pot, reduce the heat to low, and simmer the chili for 2 hours.

6. Stir in the sweet potatoes. Continue to simmer over low heat for 2 hours, then remove the beef chunks and shred with forks. Place the beef back into the Dutch oven, stir, and re-cover the pot. Cook for 25 minutes or until the flavors meld.

SPLIT PEA SOUP WITH HAM

SERVES 6
PREP TIME: 15 minutes
COOK TIME: 1 hour
DAIRY-FREE, GLUTEN-FREE, ONE POT

This split pea soup is modeled after a popular restaurant soup my husband had as a child in California. Although that specific recipe is unknown, this version showcases the creaminess of peas pureed to create a soup that is anything but ordinary.

1 tablespoon extra-virgin olive oil

1 carrot, diced

1 small white onion, diced

2 garlic cloves, minced

2½ cups Chicken Bone Broth (page 154) or store-bought

2 cups split peas, rinsed

1 teaspoon dried thyme

1 teaspoon salt

1 teaspoon freshly ground black pepper

½ teaspoon smoked paprika

4 cups water

4 ounces ham steak, diced

1. In a Dutch oven over medium heat, heat the oil. Add the carrot, onion, and garlic and cook for 5 minutes, or until slightly tender.

2. Stir in the broth, split peas, thyme, salt, pepper, and paprika and bring the soup to a simmer.

3. Cover the pot and cook for 20 minutes, or until the peas are softened.

4. Transfer 2 cups of soup to a tall container, or traditional blender, and using an immersion blender, or traditional blender, puree the soup and return it to the pot.

5. Reduce the heat to low, stir in the water and ham, and simmer for 25 minutes to meld the flavors.

VARIATION TIP: If you need to serve a vegan or vegetarian dish, leave out the ham and use Vegetable Broth (page 160) or store-bought broth instead of chicken broth.

TRADITIONAL CHICKEN
NOODLE SOUP

SERVES 4
PREP TIME: 10 minutes
COOK TIME: 40 minutes
DAIRY-FREE, ONE POT

Everyone has their favorite chicken noodle soup; this just happens to be the recipe my husband shared with me when we first met. Bright flavors and a healing broth combine to create the ideal comfort food that might just stand up to your favorite.

4 cups Chicken Bone Broth (page 154) or store-bought
3 cups water
1 pound boneless, skinless chicken breasts
4 celery stalks, diced
3 carrots, diced
1 small yellow onion, diced
4 garlic cloves, minced
1 tablespoon vegetable bouillon
1 teaspoon freshly ground black pepper, plus more as needed
1 pound egg noodles
1 bunch fresh parsley, leaves only, chopped and divided

1. In a Dutch oven over medium heat, combine the broth, water, chicken, celery, carrots, onion, garlic, bouillon, and pepper. Bring to a boil. Boil for 25 minutes, or until the chicken is cooked through.

2. Remove the chicken and shred it with two forks, then return it to the pot and add the noodles. Reserve 2 tablespoons of parsley for garnish, then add the remaining parsley to the soup.

3. Reduce the heat to low and cook for 10 minutes, or until the noodles are tender.

4. Taste and season with more pepper, as needed, and top with the reserved parsley.

MAKE-AHEAD TIP: If you want to make this in advance to freeze for later use, leave the pasta out of the soup and add it only when reheating. This prevents the pasta from soaking up too much of the liquid or becoming mushy.

WHITE BEAN ROSEMARY SOUP

SERVES 4
PREP TIME: 10 minutes
COOK TIME: 30 minutes
GLUTEN-FREE, ONE POT, VEGAN, WEEKNIGHT

This quick bean soup is a great way to get protein in your meal while remaining vegan. The brightness of the rosemary really brings out the flavor of the beans and the more subtle spices.

1 tablespoon extra-virgin olive oil

2 garlic cloves, minced

4 cups Vegetable Broth (page 160) or store-bought

2 (15-ounce) cans great northern beans, undrained

1 teaspoon dried rosemary

½ teaspoon smoked paprika

½ teaspoon salt

¼ teaspoon dried sage

⅛ teaspoon red pepper flakes

Freshly ground black pepper

1. In a Dutch oven over medium heat, heat the oil. Add the garlic and cook for 3 minutes, stirring regularly, until the garlic is lightly browned.

2. Stir in the broth, beans and their liquid, rosemary, paprika, salt, sage, and red pepper flakes. Bring the soup to a boil, reduce the heat to low, cover the pot, and simmer for 20 minutes to meld the flavors.

3. Taste and season with black pepper to serve.

VARIATION TIP: Use any white bean you prefer in this recipe. Cannellini and navy beans are also excellent choices.

6

VEGAN AND VEGETARIAN

BLACK BEAN ENCHILADA BAKE

SERVES 6
PREP TIME: 10 minutes
COOK TIME: 30 minutes
GLUTEN-FREE, ONE POT, VEGETARIAN, WEEKNIGHT

*Sometimes I want enchiladas, but I don't want to fuss with rolling them indi-
vidually. The solution is this super-easy enchilada bake using quality canned
red enchilada sauce and a perfect blend of black beans and cheese. I like to serve
these enchiladas with additional chopped fresh cilantro, shredded cheese, hot
sauce, avocado, and sour cream.*

1 (15-ounce) can black
  beans, drained
  and rinsed
1½ cups whole kernel corn
½ cup chopped
  fresh cilantro
1 jalapeño pepper, seeded
  and diced
1 teaspoon garlic powder
1 teaspoon ground cumin
12 corn tortillas
1½ cups red
  enchilada sauce
1½ cups shredded
  cheddar cheese

1. Preheat the oven to 400°F. Coat the bottom
   and sides of a Dutch oven with nonstick
   cooking spray.

2. In a medium bowl, stir together the black beans,
   corn, cilantro, jalapeño, garlic powder, and cumin
   to combine well.

3. Place 4 corn tortillas in a single layer in the
   prepared Dutch oven. Top the tortillas with
   one-third of the black bean mixture, one-third of
   the enchilada sauce, and one-third of the cheddar cheese. Repeat the layers two more times,
   ending with a layer of cheese.

4. Cover the pot and bake for 20 minutes. Remove
   the lid and bake for 10 minutes, or until lightly
   browned on top. Serve hot.

VARIATION TIP: You can also use refried black beans
in place of whole beans for a smoother texture.

CHUNKY RATATOUILLE

WITH FRESH HERBS

SERVES 6
PREP TIME: 15 minutes
COOK TIME: 45 minutes
GLUTEN-FREE, ONE POT, VEGETARIAN

Ratatouille is a delicious traditional Provençal vegetable dish packed with a variety of fresh herbs. Garlic, mellow onion, acidic tomato, and creamy eggplant combine alongside zucchini and squash to create a toothsome vegetarian meal.

5 tablespoons extra-virgin olive oil

1 yellow onion, sliced

4 garlic cloves, minced

1 medium eggplant, cut into ¼-inch slices

1 small zucchini, cut into ¼-inch slices

2 large tomatoes, chopped

1 green bell pepper, chopped

¼ cup chopped fresh oregano leaves

¼ cup chopped fresh basil leaves

2 tablespoons chopped fresh thyme leaves

½ teaspoon salt

¼ teaspoon fennel seeds

¼ cup crumbled goat cheese

2 tablespoons chopped fresh parsley (optional)

1. Preheat the oven to 425°F.

2. In a Dutch oven over medium heat, heat the oil. Add the onion and garlic and cook for 2 to 3 minutes, until nearly softened. Add the eggplant and cook for 5 minutes, or until softened. Remove from the heat and stir in the zucchini, tomatoes, bell pepper, oregano, basil, thyme, salt, and fennel seeds to combine well, spreading into an even layer.

3. Cover the pot and bake for 20 minutes. Remove the lid and cook for 15 minutes, or until browned on top.

4. Garnish with goat cheese and parsley (if using) to serve.

COOKING TIP: For added presentation appeal, layer the vegetables to create a rainbow of colors in a spiral before topping with the garlic–olive oil mixture and fresh herbs.

PUMPKIN RISOTTO

SERVES 6
PREP TIME: 15 minutes
COOK TIME: 40 minutes
GLUTEN-FREE, ONE POT, VEGETARIAN

This creamy, autumn-inspired dish combines two of my favorite things: pumpkin and risotto. The perfectly cooked rice easily complements the sweet pumpkin with the addition of peppery herbs. For even more texture and flavor, top this risotto with roasted pumpkin seeds (pepitas) and crumbled goat cheese.

1 tablespoon
   unsalted butter
1 tablespoon extra-virgin
   olive oil
1 shallot, diced
2 garlic cloves, minced
2 cups arborio rice
1 teaspoon dried rosemary
1 teaspoon salt, plus more
   as needed
1 teaspoon dried thyme
¼ teaspoon
   ground nutmeg
6 to 8 cups Vegetable
   Broth (page 160)
   or store-bought
1 cup pumpkin puree
4 ounces cream cheese
Freshly ground
   black pepper
2 tablespoons chopped
   fresh parsley (optional)

1. In a Dutch oven over medium heat, melt the butter and heat the oil. Add the shallot and garlic and cook for 2 minutes, stirring regularly, until softened.

2. Add the rice and cook for 2 to 3 minutes, until lightly browned. Stir in the rosemary, salt, thyme, and nutmeg.

3. Add 1 cup of broth to the rice and cook, stirring constantly, until the liquid is absorbed. Continue this process, adding 1 cup of broth at a time, until 6 cups have been used. This will take about 20 minutes.

4. Taste the rice to see if it is al dente. If it is not softened, continue adding liquid, ½ cup to 1 cup at a time, stirring until absorbed and checking the doneness after each addition. The rice should be just al dente, not mushy.

5. Once cooked, reduce the heat to low and stir in the pumpkin and cream cheese until heated through and combined. Taste and season with salt and pepper. Serve topped with the parsley (if using).

DEEP-DISH VEGETABLE PIZZA

SERVES 4
PREP TIME: 10 minutes
COOK TIME: 35 minutes
ONE POT, VEGETARIAN, WEEKNIGHT

It turns out that the Dutch oven is the perfect tool for making deep-dish pizza. The bottom of the crust crisps beautifully, and the top becomes lightly browned. And, because this pizza is ready in only 45 minutes, it is sure to become a weeknight favorite.

1½ tablespoons extra-virgin olive oil, divided

2 cups plain Greek yogurt

2½ cups all-purpose flour

1 teaspoon garlic powder

½ teaspoon dried basil

½ teaspoon salt

1¼ cups Tomato Basil Marinara Sauce (page 159), or store-bought

½ cup diced bell pepper

½ cup diced red onion

½ cup diced mushrooms

½ cup diced Roma tomato

¼ cup sliced black olives

1¼ cups shredded whole-milk mozzarella cheese

1. Preheat the oven to 375°F. Brush 1 tablespoon of oil over the bottom and sides of a Dutch oven and set aside.

2. In a large bowl, stir together the yogurt, flour, garlic powder, basil, and salt until a dough forms. Press the dough into the bottom of the prepared Dutch oven, so the outer rim of the dough creates a lip for the pizza crust.

3. Evenly spread the marinara sauce over the crust, leaving the rim empty.

4. Scatter the bell pepper, red onion, mushrooms, tomato, and olives over the sauce. Top with the mozzarella cheese.

5. Brush the remaining ½ tablespoon of oil onto the crust rim.

6. Bake, uncovered, for 30 to 35 minutes, until the crust has risen and is golden on the edges and the cheese melts and is bubbling. Remove and let stand for 10 minutes before cutting into slices to serve.

RED LENTIL SPINACH CURRY

SERVES 6
PREP TIME: 10 minutes
COOK TIME: 35 minutes
GLUTEN-FREE, ONE POT, VEGAN, WEEKNIGHT

By heating the spices in oil at the beginning of this recipe, you infuse the rich curry taste into the lentils, creating a nice depth of flavor that pairs well with Fluffy Jasmine Rice (page 157).

1 tablespoon extra-virgin olive oil

½ cup chopped red onion

4 garlic cloves, minced

1 tablespoon minced peeled fresh ginger

1½ teaspoons garam masala

1 teaspoon ground cumin

1 teaspoon salt

½ teaspoon smoked paprika

¼ teaspoon ground coriander

1 (14.5-ounce) can diced tomatoes

2 cups full-fat coconut milk

1 cup dried red lentils

3 cups fresh baby spinach

1. In a Dutch oven over medium heat, heat the oil. Add the onion and garlic and cook for 3 to 4 minutes, stirring regularly, until the onion is softened.

2. Stir in the ginger, garam masala, cumin, salt, paprika, and coriander to combine. Cook for about 1 minute, or until fragrant.

3. Add the tomatoes and their juices and coconut milk and bring to a boil. Reduce the heat to low, add the lentils, and continue simmering for 20 minutes, stirring occasionally.

4. Stir in the spinach and cook for 2 minutes, stirring occasionally.

VARIATION TIP: If you prefer a spicy curry, add 1 serrano chile, seeded and chopped, in step 1.

SPINACH ARTICHOKE LASAGNA

SERVES 6
PREP TIME: 20 minutes
COOK TIME: 35 minutes
ONE POT, VEGETARIAN

A simple vegetable filling layered between classic lasagna noodles creates a delicious pasta dish that is light yet satisfying. You'll love the combination of cooked spinach and artichoke hearts that give this dish an earthy flavor.

1 (14-ounce) can artichoke hearts in water, drained and chopped

1 (10-ounce) package frozen chopped spinach, thawed and drained

8 ounces cream cheese, at room temperature

8 ounces ricotta cheese

1 teaspoon garlic powder

½ teaspoon dried oregano

⅛ teaspoon red pepper flakes

10 to 12 oven-ready lasagna noodles

2 cups shredded mozzarella cheese

2 tablespoons chopped fresh parsley (optional)

1 tablespoon freshly grated Parmesan cheese (optional)

1. Preheat the oven to 400°F.

2. In a large bowl, stir together the artichoke hearts, spinach, cream cheese, ricotta, garlic powder, oregano, and red pepper flakes.

3. Coat the sides and bottom of the Dutch oven with nonstick cooking spray.

4. Lay 3 to 4 lasagna noodles over the bottom of the prepared Dutch oven and top with one-third of the spinach-cheese mixture, then one-third of the mozzarella cheese. Repeat the layers two more times, ending with a mozzarella layer on top.

5. Bake, uncovered, for 35 minutes, or until bubbling and starting to brown. Remove and let sit for 5 minutes before serving. If desired, garnish with parsley and Parmesan.

SERVING TIP: The tantalizing aromas will have you ready to dig in as soon as this lasagna is done, but don't skip the 5-minute rest before slicing and serving. That time gives the ingredients a chance to rest and firm up slightly for a prettier presentation.

MUSHROOM AND GARLIC
RISOTTO

SERVES 6
PREP TIME: 15 minutes
COOK TIME: 40 minutes
GLUTEN-FREE, ONE POT, VEGETARIAN

Risotto is one of those dishes that, once you conquer it, will make you feel like the star of the kitchen. Perfectly creamy yet al dente rice combines with rich mushrooms and garlic for an ideal side dish, though the risotto is also hearty enough to stand on its own.

1 tablespoon extra-virgin
 olive oil
8 ounces button
 mushrooms, diced
1 shallot, diced
4 garlic cloves, minced
1 tablespoon
 unsalted butter
2 cups arborio rice
1 teaspoon salt
1 teaspoon dried thyme
½ teaspoon freshly ground
 black pepper
6 to 8 cups Vegetable
 Broth (page 160)
 or store-bought
½ cup freshly grated
 Parmesan cheese, plus
 1 tablespoon
½ cup frozen peas
2 tablespoons chopped
 fresh parsley (optional)

1. In a Dutch oven over medium heat, heat the oil. Add the mushrooms, shallot, and garlic and cook for 5 minutes, stirring regularly, until the vegetables start to soften.

2. Add the butter to the pot to melt. Add the rice and cook for 2 to 3 minutes, stirring, until lightly browned.

3. Stir in the salt, thyme, and pepper, then immediately add 1 cup of broth. Cook the rice mixture, stirring constantly until the broth is absorbed. Continue this process, adding 1 cup of broth at a time, until 6 cups have been used. This will take about 20 minutes.

4. Taste the rice to see if it is al dente. If it is not softened, continue adding liquid, ½ cup to 1 cup at a time, stirring until absorbed and checking the doneness after each addition. The rice should be just al dente, not mushy.

5. Remove the Dutch oven from the heat. Stir in ½ cup of Parmesan cheese and the peas. Let sit for 5 minutes until heated through.

6. Stir the risotto before serving and top each serving with ½ teaspoon of Parmesan and parsley (if using).

VARIATION TIP: Baby bella mushrooms are a great substitute for the button mushrooms in this recipe, if preferred.

PORTABELLA MUSHROOM
POT ROAST

SERVES 6
PREP TIME: 20 minutes
COOK TIME: 1 hour 20 minutes
GLUTEN-FREE, ONE POT, VEGAN, WEEKEND

Impress your vegan and vegetarian friends with a hearty slow-cooked "pot roast" filled with classic flavors and comforting aromas. The Dutch oven allows you to cook the mushrooms and vegetables slowly to create that rich base you expect while staying true to vegan diet needs.

1½ tablespoons
   extra-virgin olive oil
1 yellow onion, chopped
4 garlic cloves, minced
2 tablespoons
   tomato paste
1 teaspoon salt
1 teaspoon freshly ground
   black pepper
2 pounds portabella
   mushrooms, sliced
2 large carrots, cut into
   1½- to 2-inch pieces
1 pound red
   potatoes, quartered
2 tablespoons fresh thyme
   leaves, chopped

1. Preheat the oven to 350°F.

2. In a Dutch oven over medium heat, combine the oil, onion, and garlic. Cook for 3 to 4 minutes, stirring regularly.

3. Stir in the tomato paste, salt, and pepper to combine.

4. Add the mushrooms, carrots, potatoes, thyme, and rosemary and stir until the vegetables are lightly coated with the tomato paste mixture. Stir in the broth, liquid aminos, and smoked paprika.

1 tablespoon fresh rose-
mary leaves, chopped

1½ cups Vegetable
Broth (page 160)
or store-bought

2 tablespoons
liquid aminos

½ teaspoon
smoked paprika

2 tablespoons chopped
fresh parsley

5. Cover the pot and bake for 45 minutes. Remove from the oven and stir well. Bake, uncovered, for 30 minutes. Serve with a sprinkle of fresh parsley.

COOKING TIP: If the sauce is too thin, add a slurry of 1 tablespoon cornstarch mixed with 1 tablespoon water to the pot, stir to combine, and cook over medium heat for 3 to 5 minutes, until thickened.

SUN-DRIED TOMATO

ARTICHOKE PASTA

SERVES 6
PREP TIME: 15 minutes
COOK TIME: 30 minutes
VEGETARIAN, WEEKNIGHT

This simple weeknight pasta dish is ideal to serve alone for a vegetarian entrée. It can also be paired with Garlic Butter Baked Halibut (page 100) or Tomato Basil Braised Chicken (page 111).

12 ounces cavatappi pasta

1 tablespoon extra-virgin olive oil

1 tablespoon unsalted butter

1 shallot, minced

2 garlic cloves, minced

¾ cup heavy (whipping) cream

½ cup whole milk

4 ounces cream cheese

1 teaspoon freshly ground black pepper

½ cup sun-dried tomatoes

1 (14-ounce) can quartered artichoke hearts in water, drained

2 tablespoons chopped fresh basil

1. Cook the pasta in a Dutch oven according to package directions until al dente. Drain and set aside, reserving ½ cup of pasta water.

2. In the same Dutch oven over medium heat, combine the oil, butter, shallot, and garlic. Cook for 3 to 4 minutes, stirring regularly.

3. Reduce the heat to low and stir in the heavy cream, milk, and reserved pasta water. Whisk in the cream cheese until combined and melted into the sauce. Simmer the sauce for 5 to 7 minutes, stirring occasionally, until thickened.

4. Add the pepper, sun-dried tomatoes, and artichoke hearts, stir well, and simmer for 2 minutes.

5. Add the cooked pasta and basil and stir until the pasta is coated completely. Let stand for 5 minutes before serving.

VARIATION TIP: If your diet allows Parmesan, replace the cream cheese with ½ cup grated Parmesan cheese.

THREE-CHEESE BAKED
MACARONI AND CHEESE

SERVES 4
PREP TIME: 15 minutes
COOK TIME: 35 minutes
VEGETARIAN

Nothing is more quintessentially comforting than macaroni and cheese. This version includes three of my favorite cheeses: cheddar, Gruyère, and Monterey Jack. Although this recipe doesn't start with a traditional roux, it is deliciously creamy and perfect for satisfying your cravings for cheesy pasta.

1 pound elbow macaroni

1 cup whole milk

8 tablespoons (1 stick) unsalted butter

1 teaspoon salt, plus more as needed

1 teaspoon freshly ground black pepper, plus more as needed

½ teaspoon dry mustard

1 cup shredded sharp cheddar cheese

½ cup shredded Gruyère cheese

½ cup shredded Monterey Jack cheese

½ cup heavy (whipping) cream

¼ cup panko bread crumbs

2 tablespoons chopped fresh parsley or fresh thyme leaves (optional)

1. Cook the macaroni in a Dutch oven according to package directions, drain, and return to the Dutch oven.

2. Stir in the milk, butter, salt, pepper, and dry mustard.

3. Stir in the cheddar, Gruyère, and Jack cheeses until melted, then stir in the heavy cream. Taste and season with additional salt or pepper, as needed. Top the macaroni and cheese with the panko bread crumbs.

4. Bake, uncovered, for 20 minutes, or until bubbling and browned. Serve topped with the parsley (if using).

VARIATION TIP: Mix and match your preferred cheeses, using at least 2 cups of cheese for best results.

SPAGHETTI SQUASH
BRUSCHETTA BAKE

SERVES 4
PREP TIME: 10 minutes
COOK TIME: 40 minutes
GLUTEN-FREE, VEGAN

In this spin on the beloved appetizer, spaghetti squash is paired with the classic flavors of garlic, tomato, and olive oil. This fiber-rich dish is vegan, low calorie, and packed with flavor. It stands on its own as a light entrée or is lovely paired with Tomato Basil Braised Chicken (page 111) for a more substantial meal.

4½ tablespoons extra-virgin olive oil, divided

1 (4-pound) spaghetti squash, halved lengthwise and seeded

1 teaspoon salt

1 teaspoon freshly ground black pepper

6 garlic cloves, unpeeled

4 Roma tomatoes, diced

¼ cup chopped fresh basil

1. Preheat the oven to 400°F.

2. Brush a Dutch oven with 1½ teaspoons of oil.

3. Brush the interior flesh of each squash half with 1½ teaspoons to 1 tablespoon of oil and sprinkle each half with ½ teaspoon of salt and ½ teaspoon of pepper.

4. Place the squash, cut-side down, in the prepared Dutch oven. Wrap the garlic cloves in a small piece of aluminum foil, seal it closed, and place it inside the Dutch oven next to the squash.

5. Bake, uncovered, for 35 to 40 minutes.

6. Remove the foil packet with the garlic from the Dutch oven. Squeeze the garlic pulp from the skins and crush or mince the roasted garlic, then toss it in a large bowl and add the tomatoes and basil.

7. Using two forks, shred the spaghetti squash. Add the strands to the tomato mixture along with the remaining 2 tablespoons of oil. Toss to coat and combine. Serve immediately.

SERVING TIP: Drizzle 1½ teaspoons balsamic vinegar reduction over each serving.

7

FISH AND SEAFOOD

BAKED HONEY DIJON SALMON

SERVES 4
PREP TIME: 5 minutes
COOK TIME: 20 minutes
DAIRY-FREE, GLUTEN-FREE, ONE POT, WEEKNIGHT

A simple combination of honey and Dijon mustard is the perfect pairing with salmon for an easy-to-bake meal. Serve alongside Creamy Mashed Potatoes (page 55) or Lemon-Garlic Green Beans (page 56) for a full meal that is light, packed with protein, and sure to satisfy.

1½ teaspoons extra-virgin olive oil

⅓ cup honey

2 tablespoons Dijon mustard

2 garlic cloves, minced

½ teaspoon salt

½ teaspoon freshly ground black pepper

4 (4-ounce) salmon fillets, skin removed

1. Preheat the oven to 400°F. Line the bottom of a Dutch oven with parchment paper. Brush the parchment paper with the oil and set aside.

2. In a small bowl, whisk the honey, mustard, garlic, salt, and pepper to blend.

3. Place the salmon fillets in the prepared Dutch oven in a single layer. Brush half of the mustard mixture over the salmon, reserving the rest for later.

4. Bake, uncovered, for 10 minutes. Gently flip the salmon fillets and brush them with the remaining honey mustard mixture. Bake for 10 minutes more, or until the internal temperature reaches 145°F. Remove and let stand for 5 minutes before serving.

COOKING TIP: For rare-cooked salmon, reduce the cooking time to 15 minutes (an internal temperature of 110° to 115°F).

CAJUN SPICED CATFISH

SERVES 4
PREP TIME: 5 minutes
COOK TIME: 15 minutes
GLUTEN-FREE, ONE POT, WEEKNIGHT

This flaky catfish has a light Cajun flavor complemented by garlic and butter. With only five ingredients, this recipe creates an ideal meal for busy weeknights. The catfish pairs beautifully with Brown Sugar and Sage Black-Eyed Peas (page 52) or Lemon-Garlic Green Beans (page 56).

1½ teaspoons extra-virgin olive oil

4 (4-ounce) catfish fillets

2 tablespoons unsalted butter

4 garlic cloves, minced

1 teaspoon Cajun seasoning

1 lemon, thinly sliced

1. Preheat the oven to 425°F. Line a Dutch oven with parchment paper. Brush the parchment paper with the oil.

2. Place the catfish fillets in the prepared Dutch oven in a single layer. Top each fillet with 1½ teaspoons of butter, one-quarter of the garlic, and ¼ teaspoon of Cajun seasoning. Top each fillet with 2 lemon slices.

3. Cover the pot and bake for 10 minutes. Remove the lid and bake for 5 minutes. Let stand for 5 minutes before serving with additional lemon slices.

VARIATION TIP: This recipe can also be made with tilapia, cod, or pollock fillets.

CRAB CAKES WITH

SPICY GARLIC AIOLI

SERVES 2
PREP TIME: 15 minutes
COOK TIME: 20 minutes
DAIRY-FREE, WEEKNIGHT

Fried in a Dutch oven to avoid splatter, these cakes are perfectly crisp on the outside and tender and flaky on the inside. Paired with an easy homemade aioli, this dish is a great appetizer for parties or a wonderful entrée that is simple to prepare and always impresses.

FOR THE CRAB CAKES

1 large egg
¼ cup mayonnaise
1 tablespoon
  Dijon mustard
1 teaspoon
  Worcestershire sauce
2 teaspoons freshly
  squeezed lemon juice
1 tablespoon chopped
  fresh parsley
2 scallions, white and
  green parts, chopped
1½ teaspoons Old
  Bay seasoning
1 pound lump crabmeat
½ cup panko
  bread crumbs
¼ cup vegetable oil
1 lemon, cut into wedges

1. **To make the crab cakes:** In a large bowl, stir together the egg, mayonnaise, mustard, Worcestershire sauce, lemon juice, parsley, scallions, Old Bay, and crab until well combined, but not overmixed. You want some chunks of crab to remain.

2. Add the bread crumbs and gently mix until combined. Divide the mixture into 6 portions and form each portion into a patty about ½ inch thick.

3. In a Dutch oven over medium heat, heat the oil until it reaches 350°F.

4. Working in batches, if needed, carefully place the crab cakes into the hot oil in a single layer and cook for 2 to 3 minutes per side, until golden brown. Transfer the crab cakes to paper towels to drain. Plate and garnish with lemon wedges.

½ cup mayonnaise

1 garlic clove, minced

1 teaspoon Dijon mustard

1 teaspoon freshly
   squeezed lemon juice

¼ to ½ teaspoon
   cayenne pepper

5. **To make the aioli:** In a small bowl, whisk the mayonnaise, garlic, mustard, lemon juice, and ¼ teaspoon of cayenne to blend. Taste and add the remaining cayenne, if needed.

6. Serve the aioli alongside the crab cakes with lemon wedges for squeezing.

VARIATION TIP: For spicier crab cakes, substitute your favorite Cajun seasoning for the Old Bay.

CRISPY POLLOCK WITH
HOMEMADE TARTAR SAUCE

SERVES 4
PREP TIME: 20 minutes
COOK TIME: 15 minutes
DAIRY-FREE, WEEKNIGHT

Using your Dutch oven to fry fish keeps the mess to a minimum while giving you the perfectly crisp exterior and tender interior you crave. You'll love the flavor of the batter paired with a simple dill tartar sauce.

FOR THE SAUCE

½ cup mayonnaise
1 teaspoon Dijon mustard
1 tablespoon dill
   pickle relish
1 tablespoon
   capers, chopped
1 teaspoon chopped
   fresh dill
⅛ teaspoon salt
⅛ teaspoon freshly ground
   black pepper
1 teaspoon freshly
   squeezed lemon juice

1. **To make the sauce:** In a medium bowl, whisk the mayonnaise, mustard, relish, capers, dill, salt, pepper, and lemon juice to blend. Cover and refrigerate until ready to serve.

2. **To make the fish:** In a Dutch oven over medium-high heat, heat 1 inch of oil to 350°F.

3. In a shallow bowl, whisk the flour, cornmeal, bread crumbs, salt, pepper, garlic powder, onion powder, paprika, and chili powder to combine.

4. In another shallow bowl, whisk the eggs and water.

1 cup vegetable oil, plus
  more as needed

½ cup all-purpose flour

½ cup cornmeal

½ cup panko
  bread crumbs

1 teaspoon salt

1 teaspoon freshly ground
  black pepper

½ teaspoon garlic powder

½ teaspoon onion powder

½ teaspoon
  smoked paprika

¼ teaspoon chili powder

2 large eggs

1 tablespoon water

2 pounds pollock, cut into
  2-inch pieces

2 lemons, sliced

5. Dip the fish into the egg mixture and then into the flour mixture, making sure each piece is coated well. Place the fish into the hot oil in a single layer, being careful not to overcrowd the pan. Cook for 2 to 3 minutes per side, until golden brown and crispy, cooked through, and flaky. Serve with the sauce and lemon slices.

COOKING TIP: Cook the fish until it reaches an internal temperature of 140° to 145°F. The fish should be flaky and no longer translucent.

GARLIC BUTTER BAKED HALIBUT

SERVES 4
PREP TIME: 5 minutes
COOK TIME: 15 minutes
GLUTEN-FREE, ONE POT, WEEKNIGHT

A hearty fish like halibut is ideal for baking in the Dutch oven. A light garlic-butter sauce adds amazing flavor to this dish and a side of Fluffy Jasmine Rice (page 157), or Creamy Mashed Potatoes (page 55) and Parmesan Pesto Bread (page 42) make it a full meal.

4 (4-ounce) halibut fillets

1 teaspoon salt

½ teaspoon freshly ground black pepper

½ teaspoon smoked paprika

8 tablespoons (1 stick) unsalted butter

4 garlic cloves, minced

1 lemon, quartered

1. Preheat the oven to 400°F. Line a Dutch oven with parchment paper.

2. Season the halibut fillets on both sides with the salt, pepper, and paprika. Place the fillets into the prepared Dutch oven in a single layer. Top each fillet with 2 tablespoons of butter and one-quarter of the garlic.

3. Bake, uncovered, for 15 minutes, or until the internal temperature reaches 145°F.

4. Serve with lemon wedges on the side.

VARIATION TIP: If halibut is not available, striped bass, cod, or flounder fillets are delicious in this recipe.

HERBY LEMON SHRIMP
WITH ASPARAGUS

SERVES 4
PREP TIME: 10 minutes
COOK TIME: 10 minutes
GLUTEN-FREE, ONE POT, WEEKNIGHT

Classic Greek flavors like bright lemon and herbs really pop when served with shrimp. Here, these flavors are paired with asparagus for an easy and speedy one-pot meal that is ideal for making in your trusty Dutch oven.

2 tablespoons extra-virgin olive oil

1 shallot, minced

4 garlic cloves, minced, divided

1 pound asparagus spears, woody ends trimmed

½ teaspoon salt, divided

½ teaspoon freshly ground black pepper, divided

1½ pounds peeled and deveined medium shrimp

¼ teaspoon dried oregano

¼ teaspoon dried basil

¼ teaspoon dried dill

¼ teaspoon onion powder

2 tablespoons unsalted butter

1 lemon, quartered

1. In a Dutch oven over medium heat, combine the oil, shallot, and garlic. Sauté for 1 minute.

2. Add the asparagus, ¼ teaspoon of salt, and ¼ teaspoon of pepper and cook for 2 minutes, stirring occasionally.

3. In a large bowl, toss together the shrimp, remaining ¼ teaspoon of salt, remaining ¼ teaspoon of pepper, oregano, basil, dill, and onion powder.

4. Move the asparagus to one side of the Dutch oven and place the butter on the other side to melt.

5. Add the seasoned shrimp and cook for about 2 minutes per side until they turn pink and are mostly cooked through. Stir the asparagus into the shrimp and cook for 1 minute. Serve with lemon wedges.

VARIATION TIP: If you have a preferred Greek seasoning blend, replace the oregano, basil, dill, and onion powder with 1 teaspoon seasoning blend.

OLIVE OIL OCEAN PERCH

SERVES 4
PREP TIME: 5 minutes
COOK TIME: 15 minutes
DAIRY-FREE, GLUTEN-FREE, ONE POT, WEEKNIGHT

This easy-to-make weeknight meal brings fresh flavor to ocean perch with parsley, lemon, and a hint of cayenne. Pair the fish with Sautéed Garlic Kale with Red Peppers (page 57) for a filling meal after a busy day.

4 (4-ounce) ocean
  perch fillets
2 tablespoons extra-virgin
  olive oil
½ teaspoon salt
½ teaspoon freshly ground
  black pepper
½ teaspoon dried oregano
¼ teaspoon
  cayenne pepper
1 lemon, sliced
1 tablespoon chopped
  fresh parsley

1. Preheat the oven to 400°F. Line a Dutch oven with parchment paper.

2. Coat the ocean perch fillets with the oil and season with the salt, black pepper, oregano, and cayenne. Place the fillets into the prepared Dutch oven in a single layer. Place the lemon slices on top of the fish.

3. Bake, uncovered, for 15 minutes, or until the fish is flaky and reaches an internal temperature of 145°F. Serve immediately with a sprinkle of chopped parsley.

VARIATION TIP: Replace the lemon with orange or grapefruit slices for a fun variation on the citrus in this dish.

PARMESAN-CRUSTED
HERBED FLOUNDER

SERVES 4
PREP TIME: 5 minutes
COOK TIME: 10 minutes
WEEKNIGHT

Using the Dutch oven to panfry flounder results in a quick and easy meal that is perfectly cooked every time. You'll find that the coating of bread crumbs and light seasoning create a flavor-packed, crispy exterior, just like you'd get at your favorite fish fry.

¼ cup vegetable oil

½ cup panko
bread crumbs

¼ cup freshly grated
Parmesan cheese

1 tablespoon chopped
fresh oregano leaves

1 teaspoon garlic powder

½ teaspoon salt

½ teaspoon freshly ground
black pepper

4 (4-ounce) flounder fillets

1. In a Dutch oven over medium heat, heat the oil.

2. In a shallow bowl, stir together the bread crumbs, Parmesan cheese, oregano, garlic powder, salt, and pepper.

3. Dredge each fillet in the bread crumb mixture and carefully place the coated fillets into the hot oil in a single layer. Cook for 3 to 4 minutes per side, until the fillets are golden brown and reach an internal temperature of 145°F. Serve immediately.

VARIATION TIP: Freshly grated Parmesan cheese has the most flavor, but you can use shelf-stable Parmesan, if fresh is not available.

SHRIMP FAJITAS WITH
AVOCADO CREMA

SERVES 4
PREP TIME: 20 minutes
COOK TIME: 15 minutes
WEEKNIGHT

Easy: Shrimp fajitas roast while you whip up a simple avocado crema. This dish has robust flavor and a slight char. These fajitas are a bit lighter than those from a restaurant, and with the bold flavors and festive colors, they are a fun option for a weeknight dinner.

FOR THE FAJITAS

1 red bell pepper, sliced

1 green bell pepper, sliced

1 red onion, sliced

½ cup sliced mushrooms

3 tablespoons extra-virgin
olive oil, divided

4 garlic cloves,
minced, divided

1½ pounds peeled and
deveined medium shrimp

1 teaspoon ground cumin

½ teaspoon salt

½ teaspoon freshly ground
black pepper

½ teaspoon
smoked paprika

¼ teaspoon dried oregano

8 small flour tortillas

1. **To make the fajitas:** Preheat the oven to 375°F.

2. In a large bowl, toss together the red bell pepper, green bell pepper, red onion, mushrooms, 1 tablespoon of oil, and half the garlic. Transfer the mixture to a Dutch oven and spread it into an even layer.

3. In a large bowl, toss the shrimp with the remaining 2 tablespoons of oil, the remaining garlic, cumin, salt, pepper, paprika, and oregano to coat and combine. Set aside.

4. Bake the vegetables, uncovered, for 10 minutes. Remove from the oven, stir, and top with the shrimp mixture. Bake, uncovered, for 5 minutes. Turn the oven to broil and broil the shrimp and vegetables for 2 minutes.

1 large avocado, halved
  and pitted

½ cup sour cream

1 garlic clove, peeled

1 tablespoon freshly
  squeezed lime juice

¼ teaspoon salt

¼ teaspoon freshly ground
  black pepper

2 tablespoons chopped
  fresh cilantro

5. **To make the crema:** While the shrimp roast, scoop the avocado flesh into a blender and add the sour cream, garlic, lime juice, salt, pepper, and cilantro. Pulse until smooth. Refrigerate until ready to use.

6. **To finish the fajitas:** Place the tortillas on a microwave-safe plate and top with ½ teaspoon to 1 teaspoon of water. Wrap the tortillas in paper towels and microwave for 30 to 40 seconds until heated through.

7. Serve the shrimp fajitas filling in the warm tortillas topped with the avocado crema.

MAKE-AHEAD TIP: The crema can be made up to 24 hours before serving. Keep refrigerated in an airtight container.

SHRIMP SCAMPI

SERVES 4
PREP TIME: 15 minutes
COOK TIME: 10 minutes
GLUTEN-FREE, ONE POT, WEEKNIGHT

A deliciously rich shrimp scampi is the pinnacle of shrimp dishes, and this one, loaded with butter, garlic, and fresh herbs, is a recipe that never fails to impress. Serve with Lemon-Garlic Green Beans (page 56) and Fluffy Jasmine Rice (page 157) for a satisfying and balanced meal.

2 tablespoons extra-virgin olive oil

4 tablespoons (½ stick) unsalted butter, divided

4 garlic cloves, minced

1 shallot, minced

½ teaspoon garlic powder

¼ teaspoon red pepper flakes

1½ pounds peeled and deveined medium shrimp

1 teaspoon salt

1 teaspoon freshly ground black pepper

¼ cup Vegetable Broth (page 160) or store-bought

1 teaspoon apple cider vinegar

1½ tablespoons freshly squeezed lemon juice

2 tablespoons chopped fresh parsley

1. In a Dutch oven over medium heat, warm the oil and add 2 tablespoons of butter to melt. Add the garlic and shallot and cook for 2 minutes, stirring regularly. Stir in the garlic powder and red pepper flakes to combine.

2. Add the shrimp, salt, and black pepper and cook for about 1 minute, or until the shrimp begin to turn pink.

3. Add the broth and vinegar and simmer for 2 minutes.

4. Stir in the remaining 2 tablespoons of butter, the lemon juice, and parsley. Remove from the heat and serve immediately.

VARIATION TIP: Experiment by replacing the vegetable broth and vinegar with ¼ cup white wine.

8

POULTRY

BRAISED CAJUN CHICKEN
LEG QUARTERS

SERVES 4
PREP TIME: 15 minutes
COOK TIME: 1 hour 5 minutes
DAIRY-FREE

This simple braised chicken dish transforms an ordinary leg quarter into a succulent cut loaded with the heat of Cajun spices. The recipe also yields a delicious braising liquid that pairs beautifully with pasta, rice, or potatoes.

4 bone-in, skin-on chicken leg quarters

½ teaspoon salt

½ teaspoon freshly ground black pepper

2 tablespoons extra-virgin olive oil

1 yellow onion, chopped

1 green bell pepper, chopped

3 garlic cloves, minced

¼ cup all-purpose flour

2 teaspoons Cajun seasoning, such as Tony Chachere's

½ teaspoon dried thyme

2 cups Chicken Bone Broth (page 154) or store-bought

2 tablespoons chopped fresh parsley (optional)

1. Preheat the oven to 375°F. Season the chicken with the salt and pepper.

2. In a Dutch oven over medium heat, heat the oil. Add the seasoned chicken and cook for 4 minutes per side, or until browned. Remove and set aside.

3. In the same Dutch oven, combine the onion, bell pepper, and garlic and cook for 3 minutes, or until nearly tender.

4. Stir in the flour, Cajun seasoning, and thyme and cook for 1 minute, or until the vegetables are coated in flour.

5. Pour in the broth and stir until the mixture is smooth and begins to thicken. Remove the Dutch oven from the heat and return the chicken to the sauce, skin-side up.

6. Cover the pot and bake for 35 minutes. Remove the lid and bake for 15 minutes, or until browned and crispy on the top. Remove from the oven and let sit for 5 minutes, then serve topped with pan sauce.

TOMATO BASIL

BRAISED CHICKEN

SERVES 4
PREP TIME: 10 minutes
COOK TIME: 30 minutes
DAIRY-FREE, GLUTEN-FREE, ONE POT, WEEKNIGHT

Nothing beats the light, fresh flavor of basil and tomato. When these ingredients are paired with tender chicken breasts, the result is a perfect meal to serve alongside your favorite garden-fresh vegetables.

1 pound boneless, skinless chicken breasts

½ teaspoon salt

½ teaspoon freshly ground black pepper

½ teaspoon dried thyme

2 tablespoons extra-virgin olive oil

4 garlic cloves, minced

1 large tomato, diced

1 cup Chicken Bone Broth (page 154) or store-bought

½ cup chopped fresh basil leaves

1. Preheat the oven to 375°F.

2. Pat the chicken dry and season it with the salt, pepper, and thyme.

3. In a Dutch oven over medium heat, heat the oil until hot but not smoking. Add the chicken and cook for 4 minutes per side, or until browned.

4. Remove the Dutch oven from the heat. Spread the garlic over the chicken. Place the tomato around and on top of the chicken and pour in the broth. Sprinkle the basil over the chicken.

5. Cover the pot and bake for 20 minutes, or until the juices run clear. Serve.

VARIATION TIP: If fresh basil is not available, substitute 2 teaspoons dried basil.

COQ AU VIN

SERVES 4
PREP TIME: 20 minutes
COOK TIME: 1 hour 40 minutes
DAIRY-FREE, GLUTEN-FREE, WEEKEND

Coq au vin is a traditional French chicken and wine dish made popular in the United States by Julia Child. This version is a simpler preparation that still provides excellent, rich flavor. Pair the chicken with roasted potatoes or Creamy Mashed Potatoes (page 55) for a hearty meal.

8 bone-in, skin-on
  chicken drumsticks
2 teaspoons salt, divided
1½ teaspoons freshly
  ground black
  pepper, divided
4 bacon slices, diced
½ yellow onion, chopped
4 garlic cloves, minced
2 tablespoons
  tomato paste
1 teaspoon dried thyme
1 cup dry red wine
1 cup Chicken Bone
  Broth (page 154)
  or store-bought
2 tablespoons chopped
  fresh parsley (optional)

1. Preheat the oven to 350°F.

2. Pat the chicken drumsticks dry and lightly season with ½ teaspoon of salt and ½ teaspoon of pepper.

3. In a Dutch oven over medium heat, cook the bacon for 5 minutes until crisp. Transfer to paper towels to drain, leaving the bacon fat in the pot.

4. In the same Dutch oven, working in batches, sear the chicken in the bacon fat for 3 minutes per side, or until browned. Remove the chicken and set aside.

5. In the Dutch oven, combine the onion and garlic and cook the for 5 minutes until softened. Stir in the tomato paste, thyme, remaining 1½ teaspoons of salt, and remaining 1 teaspoon of pepper.

6. Add the wine and broth, then deglaze the pot, scraping up any browned bits from the bottom of the pot using a wooden spoon. These flavorful bits will be incorporated into the sauce. Transfer the chicken and bacon back to the Dutch oven.

7. Cover the pot and bake for 40 minutes, or until the juices run clear. Serve 2 legs per person, garnished with parsley (if using).

CHICKEN PAPRIKASH

SERVES 4
PREP TIME: 15 minutes
COOK TIME: 40 minutes
ONE POT

A traditional dish of Hungary, this chicken is served in a tomato-based sauce that just screams comfort. With only a few ingredients needed, this meal is sure to become a staple on your menu. Serve over Fluffy Jasmine Rice (page 157) or pasta.

2 tablespoons
  vegetable oil
4 bone-in, skin-on
  chicken thighs
1 white onion, chopped
3 garlic cloves, minced
2 tablespoons
  all-purpose flour
1 tablespoon smoked
  paprika or Hungarian
  paprika (if available)
1 cup tomato sauce
¾ cup Chicken Bone
  Broth (page 154)
  or store-bought
1 tablespoon tomato paste
¼ cup sour cream

1. Preheat the oven to 400°F.

2. In a Dutch oven over medium heat, heat the oil until hot but not smoking. Add the chicken, skin-side down, and sear for 3 minutes per side. Remove the chicken and set aside.

3. In the Dutch oven, combine the onion and garlic and cook for 2 to 3 minutes, until softened. Stir in the flour and paprika to coat the vegetables.

4. Add the tomato sauce, broth, and tomato paste, then stir to combine. Return the chicken to the pot.

5. Cover the pot and bake for 25 minutes, or until the juices run clear. Remove from the oven, stir in the sour cream, and serve.

VARIATION TIP: Replace the sour cream with plain yogurt for a slightly tarter flavor.

CHICKEN POTPIE

SERVES 6
PREP TIME: 20 minutes, plus 20 minutes to chill
COOK TIME: 45 minutes
ONE POT

Chicken potpie is one of those comfort-food recipes that every family has a unique twist on. In my home, the filling is important, but it's all about the crust and how it softens with that creamy chicken inside.

FOR THE CRUST

1¼ cups all-purpose flour, plus more for dusting
½ teaspoon salt
⅓ cup vegetable shortening
3 tablespoons unsalted butter
¼ cup ice water

FOR THE FILLING

1 pound boneless, skinless chicken breasts, cut into 1-inch chunks
½ teaspoon salt
½ teaspoon freshly ground black pepper
1 tablespoon unsalted butter
1 tablespoon extra-virgin olive oil
1 shallot, diced

1. **To make the crust:** In a large bowl, combine the flour and salt. Using two forks or a pastry blender, cut in the shortening and butter until the dough is formed into pea-size crumbles. Stir in the ice water, a little at a time, until the dough begins to form, then shape it into a ball. Wrap in plastic wrap and chill for at least 20 minutes.

2. **To make the filling:** Season the chicken with the salt and pepper.

3. In a Dutch oven over medium heat, melt the butter and heat the oil. Add the chicken, shallot, and garlic and cook for 10 minutes, stirring regularly, until browned.

4. Preheat the oven to 350°F.

5. Add the flour to the Dutch oven, stirring to coat the chicken and vegetables well, then add the broth and stir to combine.

6. Stir in the carrot, celery, sage, and thyme. Reduce the heat to low and simmer the filling for 10 minutes, or until thickened. Stir in the peas and corn.

2 garlic cloves, minced

½ cup all-purpose flour

2 cups Chicken Bone
   Broth (page 154)
   or store-bought

1 carrot, diced

2 celery stalks, diced

1 teaspoon dried sage

1 teaspoon dried thyme

½ cup frozen green peas

½ cup whole kernel corn

2 tablespoons chopped
   fresh parsley (optional)

7. **To assemble:** Dust a clean work surface with a bit of flour, then roll out the dough on it until it's big enough to fit over the filling in the pot.

8. Remove the Dutch oven from the heat and gently lay the dough over the chicken mixture. Cut 2 to 3 slits in the top for venting steam.

9. Bake, uncovered, for 20 minutes, or until the filling is bubbling and the crust is golden brown. Slice and serve with a sprinkle of parsley (if using).

VARIATION TIP: Add any of your family's preferred vegetables, such as potatoes, mushrooms, broccoli, or cauliflower, to the mixture. To save time, use a refrigerated piecrust in place of homemade.

CREAMY RED PEPPER
CHICKEN PASTA

SERVES 6
PREP TIME: 10 minutes
COOK TIME: 35 minutes
ONE POT, WEEKNIGHT

Simple ingredients come together to create this surprisingly bright yet creamy pasta. Using just one pot, you can prepare a dish that is satisfying, packed with vegetables and protein, and easy to clean up.

2 tablespoons extra-virgin olive oil

1 pound boneless, skinless chicken breasts, cut into 1-inch pieces

1 red bell pepper, diced

4 garlic cloves, minced

1 teaspoon dried oregano

1 teaspoon dried thyme

2 cups Chicken Bone Broth (page 154) or store-bought

1 pound rotini pasta

1 cup heavy (whipping) cream

½ cup freshly grated Parmesan cheese

1 teaspoon salt

½ teaspoon freshly ground black pepper

2 tablespoons chopped fresh parsley (optional)

1. In a Dutch oven over medium heat, heat the oil. Add the chicken and cook for 5 minutes, stirring regularly, until browned.

2. Add the bell pepper, garlic, oregano, and thyme and stir to combine. Cook for 3 minutes, or until the bell pepper starts to soften.

3. Stir in the broth, scraping up any browned bits from the bottom of the pan with a wooden spoon.

4. Add the pasta and heavy cream. Bring the mixture to a boil. Reduce the heat to low, stir, cover the pot, and cook for 15 minutes, or until the pasta is al dente.

5. Remove the lid, stir in the Parmesan cheese, salt, and pepper and cook for 5 minutes, or until the pasta is tender and the sauce has thickened. Serve garnished with parsley (if using).

SERVING TIP: Serve with a side of fresh steamed broccoli or asparagus and an additional sprinkle of freshly grated Parmesan cheese.

COCONUT CURRY BRAISED

CHICKEN THIGHS

SERVES 4
PREP TIME: 15 minutes
COOK TIME: 1 hour 20 minutes
GLUTEN-FREE

Taking cues from the Indian subcontinent, this dish is packed with the heat of curry and the mild, rich sweetness of coconut to create a harmony of flavors.

2 tablespoons extra-virgin olive oil or coconut oil

4 bone-in, skin-on chicken thighs

½ yellow onion, diced

2 tablespoons unsalted butter

4 garlic cloves, minced

2 teaspoons curry powder

1 teaspoon salt

½ teaspoon smoked paprika

½ teaspoon ground turmeric

¼ teaspoon chili powder

1 cup Chicken Bone Broth (page 154) or store-bought

2 carrots, cut into 1-inch pieces

1 (15-ounce) can chickpeas, drained and rinsed

1 (13.5-ounce) can full-fat coconut milk

1. Preheat the oven to 375°F.

2. In a Dutch oven over medium heat, heat the oil until hot but not smoking. Add the chicken and cook for 3 minutes per side, or until browned. Remove the chicken from the pot, then add the onion, butter, and garlic. Cook for 4 minutes, or until softened.

3. Stir in the curry powder, salt, paprika, turmeric, and chili powder and cook for 1 minute, stirring, until the vegetables are tender.

4. Stir in the broth until combined. Stir in the carrots, chickpeas, and coconut milk. Return the chicken to the pot.

5. Cover the pot and bake for 1 hour. Remove the lid and turn the oven to broil. Broil the chicken for 5 minutes, or until the skin is crispy and browned.

COOKING TIP: If the sauce is thinner than you prefer, remove the chicken from the Dutch oven and simmer the sauce over medium heat for 5 to 10 minutes until reduced and thickened.

LEMON PEPPER TURKEY BREAST

SERVES 6
PREP TIME: 10 minutes
COOK TIME: 1 hour 5 minutes
DAIRY-FREE, GLUTEN-FREE, ONE POT

Turkey breast is for more than just holiday meals. This bright lemon pepper version is a great meal for any day of the week, but I find it best suited to weekend cooking, because it requires more than an hour in the oven. With only five ingredients and about as many steps, you'll love keeping this option on your menu rotation. I like to serve my turkey with Bacon-Fried Brussels Sprouts (page 50) and Creamy Mashed Potatoes (page 55).

1 (2½-pound) turkey breast

1 teaspoon freshly ground black pepper

½ teaspoon salt

1 lemon, sliced

1½ cups Chicken Bone Broth (page 154) or store-bought

1. Preheat the oven to 375°F.

2. Pat the turkey breast dry and season it with the pepper and salt. Place the breast in a Dutch oven, skin-side up, and arrange the lemon slices across the top of the breast. Pour the broth around the breast.

3. Cover the pot and bake for 1 hour, or until the internal temperature reaches 165°F. Remove the lid and turn the oven to broil. Broil the turkey breast for 5 minutes, or until golden brown.

4. Slice and serve. Remove the lemon slices from the turkey breast before serving.

COOKING TIP: For safety, use a meat thermometer to make sure the turkey breast has reached an internal temperature of 165°F before serving.

ONE-POT CHICKEN SPAGHETTI

SERVES 6
PREP TIME: 15 minutes
COOK TIME: 30 minutes
ONE POT, WEEKNIGHT

Inspired by the classic potluck dishes of my childhood, this one-pot meal is ready in under an hour and is packed with flavor. Seasoned chicken is browned, then simmered to create a rich sauce to pair with pasta and creamy pepper Jack cheese.

1 pound boneless, skinless chicken breasts, cut into 1-inch pieces

1 teaspoon ground cumin

½ teaspoon salt

¼ teaspoon freshly ground black pepper

¼ teaspoon dried oregano

3 tablespoons extra-virgin olive oil

1 green bell pepper, diced

2 garlic cloves, minced

2 cups Chicken Bone Broth (page 154) or store-bought

½ cup salsa

1 pound spaghetti, broken in half

2 cups shredded pepper Jack cheese

2 tablespoons chopped fresh cilantro (optional)

1. In a medium bowl, stir together the chicken, cumin, salt, pepper, and oregano.

2. In a Dutch oven over medium heat, heat the oil. Add the chicken, bell pepper, and garlic and cook for 5 minutes, stirring occasionally, until the chicken is browned.

3. Stir in the broth and salsa and bring the mixture to a boil.

4. Add the pasta, stir to combine, and reduce the heat to low.

5. Cover the pot and simmer for 15 minutes, or until the pasta is al dente. Remove the lid, add the pepper Jack cheese, and cook, stirring, for about 3 minutes to melt the cheese.

6. Serve topped with the cilantro (if using).

VARIATION TIP: For more heat, add a chopped jalapeño pepper with the bell pepper and garlic.

TERIYAKI CHICKEN RICE BAKE

SERVES 6
PREP TIME: 10 minutes
COOK TIME: 35 minutes
DAIRY-FREE, ONE POT, WEEKNIGHT

This bake allows flavors to meld while also creating just a bit of crisp around the edges of the rice. Loaded with vegetables as well as lean chicken breast, this meal is family friendly and perfect for using leftover rice.

2 tablespoons extra-virgin olive oil

1 pound boneless, skinless chicken breasts, cut into 1-inch chunks

2 garlic cloves, minced

1 carrot, diced

2 celery stalks, diced

½ cup soy sauce

¼ cup water

¼ cup packed brown sugar

1 tablespoon rice vinegar

1 teaspoon ground ginger

½ teaspoon salt

½ teaspoon freshly ground black pepper

3 cups cooked white rice

2 cups snow peas, strings removed

1 cup frozen peas

6 teaspoons sesame seeds

1. Preheat the oven to 400°F.

2. In a Dutch oven over medium heat, heat the oil. Add the chicken and garlic and cook for 5 minutes, stirring regularly, until the chicken is lightly browned.

3. Add the carrot and celery and cook for 2 to 3 minutes, until the vegetables start to soften.

4. Reduce the heat to low and stir in the soy sauce, water, brown sugar, vinegar, ginger, salt, and pepper. Cook for 5 minutes, stirring, until the vegetables are tender. Remove from the heat and stir in the rice, snow peas, and frozen peas and spread the mixture into an even layer.

5. Bake, uncovered, for 20 minutes, or until the rice is cooked through and the top is slightly browned. Garnish each serving with 1 teaspoon of sesame seeds.

MAKE-AHEAD TIP: Follow steps 2 to 4 to prepare the mixture for baking, then transfer it to a dated and labeled freezer storage container and freeze for up to 4 months. Thaw in the refrigerator overnight, then transfer to a Dutch oven and bake as directed in step 5.

WHOLE ROASTED CHICKEN

SERVES 6
PREP TIME: 20 minutes
COOK TIME: 1 hour 35 minutes
GLUTEN-FREE, ONE POT, WEEKEND

Nothing beats a tender, juicy roasted chicken fresh from the oven. This simple recipe includes a delicious garlic butter coating and fresh herbs that slowly season the chicken from the inside out.

8 tablespoons (1 stick) unsalted butter, at room temperature

6 garlic cloves, 3 minced and 3 mashed, divided

1 teaspoon salt

1 teaspoon freshly ground black pepper

½ yellow onion, chopped

2 rosemary sprigs

1 lemon, quartered

1 (2-pound) whole chicken, cleaned and giblets removed

1. Preheat the oven to 400°F.

2. In a small bowl, stir together the butter, minced garlic, salt, and pepper. Set aside.

3. Stuff the onion, rosemary, mashed garlic, and lemon into the chicken's cavity. Place the chicken into a Dutch oven, breast-side up, and spread the garlic butter mixture all over the outside of the bird and under the skin.

4. Cover the pot and roast for 45 minutes. Remove the lid and baste the chicken with the pan juices. Roast, uncovered, for 45 minutes, or until the skin is crispy and the internal temperature reaches 165°F. Baste again with the pan juices.

5. Turn the oven to broil and broil the chicken for 5 minutes, or until browned. Let the bird rest for 10 minutes before removing the onion, rosemary, garlic, and lemon from the cavity. Slice the chicken and serve it with your favorite sides.

VARIATION TIP: For a different flavor profile, in step 2, add ½ teaspoon chili powder and ½ teaspoon cumin to the butter and omit the rosemary from the bird's cavity.

9

CHAPTER NINE

MEAT

BARBECUE PULLED PORK

SERVES 6
PREP TIME: 15 minutes
COOK TIME: 3 hours 45 minutes
DAIRY-FREE, ONE POT, WEEKEND

Slowly roasted pork shoulder is perfect for the Dutch oven, where it can be seared and then braised, creating a tender and juicy pork perfect for shredding. Serve it on whole wheat buns with a side of slaw and you'll have barbecue perfection.

½ cup packed brown
   sugar, divided

1 teaspoon salt

1 teaspoon garlic powder

1 teaspoon onion powder

½ teaspoon chili powder

½ teaspoon
   smoked paprika

½ teaspoon ground cumin

3 to 4 pounds boneless
   pork shoulder

2 tablespoons
   vegetable oil

1 white onion, chopped

1 cup Chicken Bone
   Broth (page 154) or
   store-bought, divided

1 cup ketchup

¼ cup apple cider vinegar

¼ cup yellow mustard

2 tablespoons
   Worcestershire sauce

1. Position a rack in the middle of the oven and preheat the oven to 350°F.

2. In a small bowl, stir together ¼ cup of brown sugar, the salt, garlic powder, onion powder, chili powder, smoked paprika, and cumin. Coat the outside of the pork with half of the spice mixture. Set aside the remaining spice mixture.

3. In a Dutch oven over medium heat, heat the oil until hot. Add the pork and sear for 2 minutes on all sides. Remove the Dutch oven from the heat.

4. Around the pork, place the chopped onion and pour in ½ cup of broth.

5. Cover the pot and bake on the middle rack for 3 hours.

6. In a medium bowl, stir together the remaining ¼ cup of brown sugar, reserved spice mixture, remaining ½ cup of broth, ketchup, vinegar, mustard, and Worcestershire sauce. Pour the sauce over the pork shoulder, re-cover the pot, and cook for 30 minutes to heat through.

7. Shred the pork and stir it into the sauce and drippings in the Dutch oven before serving.

BEEF LO MEIN

SERVES 4
PREP TIME: 10 minutes, plus 20 minutes to marinate
COOK TIME: 30 minutes
DAIRY-FREE

This easy beef lo mein is a delicious pasta dish inspired by Chinese cuisine. Although I love a good take-out meal, I much prefer making this dish at home where I can infuse it with big flavors using soy, brown sugar, rice vinegar, garlic, and a dash of fish sauce.

½ cup packed brown sugar

¼ cup soy sauce

2 tablespoons sesame oil

2 tablespoons mirin

2 tablespoons fish sauce

2 tablespoons extra-virgin olive oil, divided

1 tablespoon rice vinegar

3 garlic cloves, minced

½ teaspoon salt

½ teaspoon freshly ground black pepper

½ teaspoon ground ginger

1 pound rib-eye steak, thinly sliced

1 pound lo mein noodles or spaghetti

1 zucchini, julienned

1 carrot, julienned

1 yellow onion, sliced

1 cup shredded cabbage

2 tablespoons sesame seeds

1. In a large bowl, whisk the brown sugar, soy sauce, sesame oil, mirin, fish sauce, 1 tablespoon of olive oil, the rice vinegar, garlic, salt, pepper, and ginger to blend. Add the sliced rib eye, toss well, and cover with plastic wrap. Set aside for 20 minutes.

2. In a Dutch oven, cook the pasta according to the package directions, drain, and set aside.

3. In the same Dutch oven over medium heat, heat the remaining 1 tablespoon of olive oil. Add the rib eye, reserving the marinade. Cook the rib eye for 3 to 4 minutes, until browned nicely, then add the remaining marinade and simmer for 5 minutes, making sure the liquid comes to a boil.

4. Add the zucchini, carrot, onion, and cabbage. Cook for 3 minutes, tossing everything together, until just softened.

5. Add the cooked pasta and toss to coat with the sauce and mix well with the cooked vegetables and beef. Serve with a sprinkle of sesame seeds on top.

MAKE-AHEAD TIP: The beef can be marinated for up to 24 hours before cooking.

BEEF ROAST WITH
ROOT VEGETABLES

SERVES 6
PREP TIME: 20 minutes
COOK TIME: 4 hours 15 minutes
DAIRY-FREE, ONE POT, WEEKEND

Inspired by the Sunday dinners of my childhood, this beef roast meal is packed with tender beef, carrots, onions, potatoes, and a richness that comes only from allowing fats to render slowly in the oven. Simple yet decadent in its own right, this meal is fit for royalty.

½ cup all-purpose flour

1 teaspoon seasoned salt

1 teaspoon freshly ground
   black pepper

1 (3-pound) beef
   chuck roast

2 tablespoons
   vegetable oil

1 yellow onion, chopped

4 garlic cloves, mashed

1 cup beef broth

4 Yukon Gold potatoes, cut
   into 1-inch pieces

3 large carrots, cut into
   1-inch pieces

1. Position a rack in the middle of the oven and preheat the oven to 375°F.

2. In a large shallow bowl, stir together the flour, seasoned salt, and pepper.

3. Dredge the roast in the flour mixture to lightly coat it.

4. In a Dutch oven over medium heat, heat the oil until hot but not smoking. Place the roast into the pan and sear for 3 minutes per side, including top, bottom, and all sides. Remove the pot from the heat and place the onion and garlic around the sides of the beef. Pour the broth over the onion and garlic.

5. Cover the pot and roast on the middle rack for 2 hours.

6. Remove the lid, carefully flip the roast, add the potatoes and carrots, and re-cover the pot. Roast for 2 hours, or until the roast is tender and falling apart.

7. Remove and let cool for 10 minutes before shredding or slicing. Serve with the potatoes, carrots, and pan juices.

COOKING TIP: If there are enough pan juices remaining after removing the roast and vegetables, whisk ¼ cup of flour with ½ cup of pan juices until no lumps remain, then pour it into the Dutch oven with the rest of the pan juices. Bring to a simmer over medium heat and cook for 5 minutes to create a gravy for serving. Season to taste with salt and pepper and add more broth if you prefer a thinner gravy.

BRAISED SHORT RIBS

SERVES 4
PREP TIME: 10 minutes
COOK TIME: 2 hours
DAIRY-FREE, GLUTEN-FREE, WEEKEND

Braised short ribs are the perfect vehicle to showcase your cooking skills and the versatility of your Dutch oven. In this recipe, a tender cut of beef rib is braised to seal in flavor and allow the meat to tenderize. Paired with a simple sauce, the meat speaks for itself.

5 pounds beef short ribs, cut into 3- to 4-inch pieces
1 teaspoon salt
½ teaspoon freshly ground black pepper
2 tablespoons vegetable oil
1 yellow onion, chopped
4 garlic cloves, minced
2 tablespoons tomato paste
½ teaspoon dried thyme
½ teaspoon dried rosemary
½ teaspoon dried oregano
2 cups beef broth

1. Preheat the oven to 350°F.

2. Season the ribs with the salt and pepper.

3. In a Dutch oven over medium heat, heat the oil. Working in batches, brown the ribs on each side for 2 minutes, until all have been browned, leaving the drippings in the pot.

4. In the drippings, combine the onion and garlic and cook for 3 minutes, or until softened.

5. Stir in the tomato paste, thyme, rosemary, and oregano to combine. Whisk in the broth. Gently place the ribs back in the pot.

6. Cover the pot and bake for 1½ hours, or until the meat is tender.

7. Remove the ribs from the pan and heat the drippings over medium heat on the stovetop until boiling. Reduce the heat to low and simmer for 8 to 10 minutes, stirring occasionally, until thickened. Serve the ribs with the pan sauce.

VARIATION TIP: Replace ½ cup of broth with red wine for a richer flavor.

SIRLOIN TIPS WITH

MUSHROOM GRAVY

SERVES 4
PREP TIME: 15 minutes
COOK TIME: 25 minutes
WEEKNIGHT

A simple, quick meal of sirloin and mushrooms is a fantastic way to end a hectic day. Seared beef tips pair wonderfully with the earthy richness of a quick mushroom gravy. Serve atop Creamy Mashed Potatoes (page 55) or Fluffy Jasmine Rice (page 157).

1 (2-pound) beef loin tip steak, cut into 1-inch pieces

1 teaspoon salt

1 teaspoon freshly ground black pepper

½ teaspoon smoked paprika

2 tablespoons extra-virgin olive oil

2 tablespoons unsalted butter

8 ounces button mushrooms, diced

1 shallot, diced

2 garlic cloves, minced

¼ cup all-purpose flour

1 tablespoon tomato paste

2 cups beef broth

1 tablespoon Worcestershire sauce

2 tablespoons chopped fresh parsley (optional)

1. Season the beef with the salt, pepper, and paprika.

2. In a Dutch oven over medium heat, heat the oil. Add the beef to the pot and cook for 5 to 6 minutes, stirring regularly, until browned. Remove the beef from the pan and set aside.

3. Place the butter in the Dutch oven to melt. Add the mushrooms, shallot, and garlic and cook for 5 minutes, stirring regularly, until softened.

4. Stir in the flour, coating the vegetables, and cook for 1 minute. Add the tomato paste and stir to combine.

5. Stir in the broth and Worcestershire sauce. Cook for 5 minutes, stirring regularly, until the sauce has thickened.

6. Add the beef to the gravy and cook for 2 to 3 minutes, until heated through. Serve topped with parsley (if using).

INGREDIENT TIP: If available, substitute porcini mushrooms for the button mushrooms for a nuttier flavor.

ONE-POT CHILI MAC

SERVES 4
PREP TIME: 15 minutes
COOK TIME: 40 minutes
ONE POT

Boxed dinners have no place in your pantry when you can easily whip up this simple chili macaroni. A kid favorite, this chili mac is the ultimate fast-and-easy comfort-food dinner and is loaded with rich meat chili served over a cheesy pasta.

8 ounces elbow macaroni

2 tablespoons
vegetable oil

1 pound ground beef

½ yellow onion, diced

2 garlic cloves, minced

1 (14.5-ounce) can
diced tomatoes

1 cup tomato sauce

2 tablespoons
tomato paste

1 tablespoon beef bouillon

1 teaspoon ground cumin

1 teaspoon
smoked paprika

1 teaspoon chili powder

1 (15-ounce) can kidney
beans, drained
and rinsed

1 (15-ounce) can chili
beans, drained
and rinsed

2 cups shredded cheddar
cheese, divided

1. In a Dutch oven, cook the elbow macaroni according to the package directions, drain, and set aside.

2. In the Dutch oven over medium heat, heat the oil. Add the ground beef, onion, and garlic and cook for 5 minutes, or until the beef is browned.

3. Add the tomatoes and their juices, tomato sauce, tomato paste, beef bouillon, cumin, paprika, and chili powder. Stir to combine, then bring the chili to a boil.

4. Stir in the kidney beans and chili beans, reduce the heat to low, and simmer for 15 minutes, or until the chili begins to thicken.

5. Stir in the cooked macaroni and 1 cup of cheddar cheese. Remove from the heat and let stand for 5 minutes before serving with the remaining 1 cup of cheese scattered on top.

VARIATION TIP: For a healthier version, use ground turkey or ground chicken in place of the beef. You can also use reduced-fat cheese, if desired.

RIGATONI WITH PORK
SAUSAGE AND KALE

SERVES 4
PREP TIME: 10 minutes
COOK TIME: 40 minutes

The secret to this variation on a classic dish is the kale, which adds the nutrition you desire while imparting a slightly bitter flavor that complements the rich sausage for a hearty meal that is not too heavy.

1 pound rigatoni pasta

2 tablespoons extra-virgin olive oil

1 pound Italian pork sausage, casings removed

2 garlic cloves, minced

4 cups torn (small pieces) kale

1 cup Chicken Bone Broth (page 154) or store-bought

½ cup freshly grated Parmesan cheese

½ teaspoon salt

½ teaspoon freshly ground black pepper

2 tablespoons chopped fresh parsley (optional)

1. In a Dutch oven, cook the rigatoni according to the package directions, drain, and set aside.

2. In the Dutch oven over medium heat, heat the oil. Add the sausage and garlic and cook for 4 to 5 minutes, until they start to brown.

3. Add the kale and cook for 3 minutes, or until wilted.

4. Stir in the broth, scraping up any browned bits from the bottom of the pot with a wooden spoon. Reduce the heat to low and simmer for 10 minutes.

5. Add the cooked rigatoni, Parmesan cheese, salt, and pepper, then stir to combine. Simmer for 2 to 3 minutes to melt the Parmesan. Serve garnished with parsley (if using).

VARIATION TIP: To add extra heat, choose a spicy Italian sausage or add ½ teaspoon red pepper flakes in step 5.

BAKED LASAGNA
WITH MEAT SAUCE

SERVES 8
PREP TIME: 20 minutes
COOK TIME: 2 hours 15 minutes
WEEKEND

Slowly cooking this rustic meat sauce ensures your lasagna is packed with the best flavor possible. Rich meat, tender vegetables, creamy cheese, and just the right noodle-to-sauce ratio create a favorite weekend meal.

2 tablespoons extra-virgin olive oil

1 yellow onion, diced

6 garlic cloves, minced

2 pounds ground beef

1 (28-ounce) can diced tomatoes

1 (15-ounce) can tomato sauce

1½ cups beef broth

1 (6-ounce) can tomato paste

1 teaspoon dried oregano

1 teaspoon dried thyme

1 teaspoon dried basil

1 teaspoon salt

½ teaspoon freshly ground black pepper

1 (16-ounce) container ricotta cheese

1. In a Dutch oven over medium heat, heat the oil. Add the onion and garlic and cook for 3 minutes, or until softened.

2. Add the ground beef and cook for 5 minutes, or until mostly browned.

3. Stir in the tomatoes and their juices, tomato sauce, broth, tomato paste, oregano, thyme, basil, salt, and pepper to combine well. Reduce the heat to low.

4. Cover the pot and simmer for 1 hour, stirring occasionally, until thickened. Transfer the sauce to a large bowl.

5. In a medium bowl, stir together the ricotta and mozzarella cheeses, parsley, and garlic powder, until blended.

6. Preheat the oven to 375°F.

7. In the same Dutch oven, spread ½ cup of sauce into the bottom to coat it, then add 3 or 4 lasagna noodles in a single layer.

2 cups shredded
  mozzarella cheese
2 tablespoons
  dried parsley
1 teaspoon garlic powder
10 to 12 oven-ready
  lasagna noodles
2 tablespoons grated Par-
  mesan cheese (optional)

8. Spoon one-third of the sauce over the noodles. Spread one-third of the cheese mixture over the sauce. Cover the cheese with another layer of noodles, then sauce and cheese again. Repeat this once more for a total of three layers, ending with a layer of cheese.

9. Cover the pot and bake for 45 minutes. Remove the lid and bake for 15 minutes, or until browned and bubbling. Serve hot with a sprinkle of Parmesan (if using).

VARIATION TIP: Try Italian sausage in place of the ground beef for deeper flavor.

PRIME RIB OF BEEF

SERVES 6
PREP TIME: 2 hour 30 minutes
COOK TIME: 2 hours
GLUTEN-FREE, WEEKEND

Although prime rib is certainly not an everyday meal, the Dutch oven can transform your oven into a gourmet kitchen for the holidays with this simple and perfectly cooked prime rib of beef. I created this easy method so this cut of meat becomes an approachable feast for even the most novice cook, yielding tender, juicy meat every time.

1 (6-pound) standing prime rib roast

8 tablespoons (1 stick) unsalted butter, at room temperature

4 garlic cloves, minced

2 rosemary sprigs, leaves removed and chopped

2 teaspoons salt

1 teaspoon freshly ground black pepper

1. Bring the roast to room temperature for 2 hours before preparing it, loosely covered on the counter. Pat the outside of the roast dry.

2. Preheat the oven to 500°F.

3. In a small bowl, stir together the butter, garlic, rosemary, salt, and pepper. In a Dutch oven, spread half of the butter mixture onto the bottom of the pan.

4. Place the roast into the pot on the butter spread, then rub the remaining butter mixture over the outside of the roast.

5. Cover the pot and roast for 30 minutes. Remove the lid, baste the roast with the pan juices, and re-cover the pot. Reduce the heat to 250°F. Roast for 30 minutes.

6. Remove the lid, check the internal temperature, and baste the roast with the pan juices. Repeat this process every 30 minutes for a total of three times, or until the internal temperature of the roast reaches 118°F.

7. Remove from the oven and uncover the pot. Let the roast rest for 20 minutes before slicing to serve. The internal temperature should reach 125°F for a perfect medium-rare cook.

COOKING TIP: When making prime rib of beef, a meat thermometer is a must-have investment. This will help save you from overcooking what should be a perfectly cooked cut of beef.

ROASTED PORK LOIN
WITH APPLES

SERVES 4
PREP TIME: 15 minutes
COOK TIME: 1 hour
DAIRY-FREE, GLUTEN-FREE, ONE POT

Making tender, juicy pork loin is easier than ever with this simple Dutch oven preparation. A quick sear before baking keeps the juices in, while adding a nice texture to the pork that pairs well with the tender apples.

2 to 2½ pounds pork
  loin, trimmed
½ teaspoon salt
½ teaspoon freshly ground
  black pepper
2 tablespoons extra-virgin
  olive oil
1 yellow onion, chopped
½ cup Chicken Bone
  Broth (page 154)
  or store-bought
2 garlic cloves, minced
¼ cup packed brown sugar
½ teaspoon dried oregano
½ teaspoon
  smoked paprika
Pinch red pepper flakes
4 Honeycrisp apples,
  peeled, cored,
  and quartered

1. Preheat the oven to 400°F.

2. Season the pork with the salt and pepper.

3. In a Dutch oven over medium heat, heat the oil. Add the pork and sear for 2 to 3 minutes on all sides, until browned. Remove from the heat and add the onion, broth, and garlic.

4. Cover the pot and roast for 30 minutes.

5. Meanwhile, in a small bowl, stir together the brown sugar, oregano, smoked paprika, and red pepper flakes.

6. Remove the lid and sprinkle the brown sugar seasoning blend over the pork loin. Spoon a bit of the pan juices over the seasoning blend, just enough to moisten it. Place the apple pieces around the pork. Re-cover the pot and roast for 20 minutes, or until the pork reaches an internal temperature of 140°F and the apples are tender. Remove and let cool for 10 minutes before serving with the apples and pan juices.

SHREDDED BEEF TACOS

SERVES 6
PREP TIME: 10 minutes
COOK TIME: 4 hours
DAIRY-FREE, GLUTEN-FREE, ONE POT, WEEKEND

Home taco night can be so much more than just ground beef and generic spices. Slow-roasting beef in your Dutch oven creates the base for a flavor-packed taco you can serve to rave reviews.

1 cup beef broth

1 (4-ounce) can diced
    green chiles

4 garlic cloves, minced

1½ teaspoons
    ground cumin

1 teaspoon salt

½ teaspoon chili powder

½ teaspoon dried oregano

1 (2-pound) beef
    chuck roast

12 corn tortillas

Favorite taco toppings

1. Preheat the oven to 350°F.

2. In a small bowl, whisk the broth, green chiles and their juices, garlic, cumin, salt, chili powder, and oregano to blend.

3. Place the roast into the Dutch oven, then pour the broth mixture over the top.

4. Cover the pot and bake for 2 hours. Remove the lid, flip the roast, and spoon the pan juices over the top. Re-cover the pot and cook for 2 hours, or until the beef is tender and falling apart. Shred and serve with the tortillas and your favorite taco toppings.

SERVING TIP: This meat is perfect on corn tortillas, flour tortillas, or even as part of a "burrito bowl." Add your favorite toppings such as diced onion, salsa, sour cream, shredded cheese, or lime wedges for squeezing.

DESSERT

BAKED APPLE DUMPLINGS

SERVES 4
PREP TIME: 15 minutes
COOK TIME: 25 minutes
ONE POT, VEGETARIAN, WEEKNIGHT

This comforting dessert is that one recipe every home cook should have in their repertoire. Simple ingredients and preparation turn into a breathtaking display of crisp puff pastry on the outside and tender cooked sweet apple on the inside.

4 Granny Smith apples, peeled and cored

1 cup (2 sticks) unsalted butter, at room temperature

½ cup packed brown sugar

1 teaspoon ground cinnamon

¼ teaspoon ground nutmeg

1 sheet puff pastry

4 teaspoons granulated sugar

1 cup vanilla ice cream

4 tablespoons caramel syrup

1. Preheat the oven to 400°F. Line the bottom of a Dutch oven with parchment paper and set aside.

2. In a small bowl, stir together the butter, brown sugar, cinnamon, and nutmeg until well combined.

3. On a clean work surface, unfold the puff pastry and cut it into 4 equal pieces. Place a single apple onto each piece of puff pastry, positioning it in the middle.

4. Divide the butter mixture into 4 equal portions, then lightly coat the outside of each apple with the mixture and stuff at least 1 teaspoon of the mixture inside each apple.

5. Pull the sides of the puff pastry up and over the sides and top of the apple. Crimp the edges so the pastry completely encloses the apple. Place the covered apples into the prepared Dutch oven, making sure they are evenly spaced with at least 2 inches between them.

6. Sprinkle the top of each apple with 1 teaspoon of granulated sugar.

7. Bake, uncovered, for 25 minutes, or until the pastry is golden brown. Remove and let the apples rest for 10 minutes before serving with a scoop of vanilla ice cream and a drizzle of caramel syrup over the top.

SERVING TIP: Cinnamon ice cream or butter pecan ice cream is also an excellent option to serve with this hot apple dumpling.

CARAMEL PECAN BARS

SERVES 6
PREP TIME: 10 minutes
COOK TIME: 35 minutes
ONE POT, VEGETARIAN, WEEKNIGHT

Caramel and pecan are a classic pairing, and this buttery bar makes the ideal base for these flavors. Because the batter is fast and easy to prepare, this is a perfect dessert to serve to last-minute guests when you have limited supplies on hand.

1 cup all-purpose flour
½ cup sugar
1 teaspoon baking powder
½ teaspoon salt
½ cup heavy (whipping) cream
8 tablespoons (1 stick) unsalted butter, melted
2 large eggs
1 teaspoon vanilla extract
½ cup pecan pieces
12 caramel candies, cut into small pieces
¼ cup caramel syrup (optional)

1. Preheat the oven to 375°F. Line a Dutch oven with parchment paper and lightly spray it with nonstick cooking spray.

2. In a large bowl, whisk the flour, sugar, baking powder, and salt to combine.

3. In a small bowl, whisk the heavy cream, melted butter, eggs, and vanilla until combined. Stir the wet ingredients into the dry ingredients, then fold in the pecans and caramel candies. Transfer the batter to the prepared Dutch oven.

4. Bake, uncovered, for 35 minutes, or until a toothpick inserted in the center comes out clean.

5. Serve hot with a drizzle of caramel sauce (if using).

VARIATION TIP: You can also use ½ cup caramel bites instead of caramel candies. This ingredient is often found in the baked goods section of your grocery store.

CHERRY DUMP CAKE

SERVES 8
PREP TIME: 10 minutes
COOK TIME: 50 minutes
ONE POT, VEGETARIAN

This easy cake recipe uses canned pie filling, but amps things up with a home-made topping that is buttery, moist, and better than any boxed mix you've ever tasted.

1¼ cups (2½ sticks)
   unsalted butter, at
   room temperature
3 large eggs
1 tablespoon
   vanilla extract
1 cup whole milk
¼ cup heavy
   (whipping) cream
2¼ cups all-purpose flour
1 cup granulated sugar
1 tablespoon
   baking powder
1 teaspoon salt
2 (21-ounce) cans cherry
   pie filling
Powdered sugar,
   for dusting

1. Preheat the oven to 350°F. Coat a Dutch oven with nonstick cooking spray and set aside.

2. In a large bowl, using a handheld mixer, beat together the butter, eggs, and vanilla, then stir in the milk and heavy cream until combined.

3. Sift in the flour, granulated sugar, baking powder, and salt and mix until just combined. Spread the pie filling in the Dutch oven, then top with the cake batter. Stir the mixture together slightly so it is not completely incorporated but swirled.

4. Cover the pot and bake for 30 minutes. Remove the lid and bake for 20 minutes, or until browned on top.

5. Serve hot with a dusting of powdered sugar.

VARIATION TIP: The same process can be used for any canned pie filling combination you prefer.

CHOCOLATE WALNUT
BROWNIES

SERVES 6
PREP TIME: 15 minutes
COOK TIME: 35 minutes
ONE POT, VEGETARIAN

A decadent fudgy brownie is the ultimate in sweet treats. This recipe features crunch from walnuts and chocolate chunks in each bite. Kids and adults love these indulgent brownies, and it's our secret how easy they are to make.

8 tablespoons (1 stick) unsalted butter, melted
½ cup packed brown sugar
½ cup granulated sugar
2 large eggs
1 tablespoon vegetable oil
1 tablespoon vanilla extract
½ cup all-purpose flour
½ cup unsweetened cocoa powder
½ teaspoon salt
¼ cup walnut pieces
¼ cup milk chocolate chunks

1. Preheat the oven to 350°F. Line a Dutch oven with parchment paper and lightly coat it with nonstick cooking spray.

2. In a medium bowl, whisk the melted butter, brown sugar, granulated sugar, eggs, oil, and vanilla to blend.

3. Sift the flour, cocoa powder, and salt into the wet ingredients, then gently stir to combine.

4. Fold in the walnuts and chocolate chunks. Spread the batter into the prepared Dutch oven.

5. Bake, uncovered, for 35 minutes, or until a tooth-pick inserted in the center comes out clean. The brownies will be fudgy and not dry, so they may seem slightly underdone. Remove and cool for 15 minutes before slicing to serve.

VARIATION TIP: Substitute pecans for the walnuts and chocolate chips for the chocolate chunks in equal amounts, if preferred.

CINNAMON RAISIN BREAD

PUDDING WITH VANILLA GLAZE

SERVES 6
PREP TIME: 10 minutes
COOK TIME: 40 minutes
ONE POT, VEGETARIAN

This bread pudding recipe uses slightly stale cinnamon raisin bread as a base, which is topped with a decadent homemade vanilla glaze. If your bread isn't stale, bake it at 300°F for 10 minutes to dry it out.

2 cups whole milk

1¼ cups heavy (whipping) cream, divided

4 large eggs, beaten

2 tablespoons vanilla extract, divided

1½ teaspoons ground cinnamon

¼ teaspoon ground nutmeg

1 loaf stale cinnamon raisin bread, torn into pieces

½ cup raisins

2 cups powdered sugar

2 tablespoons unsalted butter, melted

¼ cup caramel syrup (optional)

1. Preheat the oven to 375°F. Coat the sides and bottom of a Dutch oven with nonstick cooking spray and set aside.

2. In a large bowl, whisk the milk, 1 cup of heavy cream, the eggs, 1 tablespoon of vanilla, the cinnamon, and nutmeg to blend.

3. In the Dutch oven, spread the bread and raisins into an even layer, then pour the milk mixture over the bread and raisins, making sure all of the bread is coated well.

4. Cover the pot and bake for 25 minutes. Remove the lid and bake for 15 minutes, or until the pudding is browned and a toothpick inserted into the center comes out clean.

5. In a small bowl, whisk the powdered sugar, remaining ¼ cup of heavy cream, the melted butter, and remaining 1 tablespoon of vanilla until a smooth glaze forms. Set aside.

6. Remove the bread pudding from the oven and immediately pour the glaze over the top. Serve hot with a drizzle of caramel sauce (if using).

FRESH PEACH COBBLER

SERVES 6
PREP TIME: 20 minutes
COOK TIME: 45 minutes
ONE POT, VEGETARIAN

With fresh ripe peaches and a perfectly flaky crust, this is the ultimate in fruit desserts. This recipe is based on the one my granny made and is ideal served hot from the oven topped with fresh whipped cream or ice cream.

FOR THE FILLING

8 medium peaches, peeled and sliced

½ cup water

6 tablespoons (¾ stick) unsalted butter, diced

¼ cup granulated sugar

2 tablespoons packed brown sugar

1 tablespoon cornstarch

1 tablespoon vanilla extract

½ teaspoon ground cinnamon

¼ teaspoon salt

FOR THE TOPPING

1¼ cups all-purpose flour

9 tablespoons (1 stick plus 1 tablespoon) cold unsalted butter

1 tablespoon granulated sugar

½ teaspoon salt

¼ cup ice water

1. **To make the filling:** Preheat the oven to 375°F.

2. In a Dutch oven, stir together the peaches, water, butter, granulated sugar, brown sugar, cornstarch, vanilla, cinnamon, and salt.

3. **To make the topping:** In a large bowl, combine the flour, cold butter, sugar, and salt. Using two forks or a pastry blender, blend the ingredients until the dough is formed into pea-size crumbles. Stir in the ice water until a dough forms. Drop half the dough, by the spoonful, into the Dutch oven over the peach mixture. Stir to combine so part of the dough is incorporated into the peach mixture. Drop the remaining dough onto the top of the peaches.

4. Cover the pot and bake for 25 minutes. Remove the lid and bake for 20 minutes more, or until bubbling and browned on top.

> **MAKE-AHEAD TIP:** Prepare the dough for the topping ahead and refrigerate for up to 3 days before using.

MIXED BERRY CRISP

SERVES 6
PREP TIME: 10 minutes
COOK TIME: 35 minutes
ONE POT, VEGETARIAN, WEEKNIGHT

Berry crisp is a great example of a classic dish made simple in the Dutch oven. The slightly sweet-tart berries and crumbly topping combine with just the right amount of sugar and spices to create a rich dessert. The crisp is ideal for topping with your favorite ice cream for a combination of textures and temperatures.

8 tablespoons (1 stick)
   unsalted butter plus
   1 tablespoon
2 cups strawberries
1 cup blueberries
1 cup blackberries
½ cup raspberries
1½ tablespoons
   cornstarch
¼ cup granulated sugar
¼ teaspoon nutmeg
Grated zest of 1 lemon
2 tablespoons freshly
   squeezed lemon juice
1 cup all-purpose flour
¾ cup rolled oats
¼ cup packed brown sugar
½ teaspoon salt

1. Preheat the oven to 400°F. Use 1 tablespoon of butter to lightly coat the bottom and sides of a 5-quart Dutch oven.

2. In the prepared Dutch oven, stir together the strawberries, blueberries, blackberries, raspberries, cornstarch, granulated sugar, nutmeg, lemon zest, and lemon juice until the berries are coated well.

3. In a large bowl, stir together the flour, oats, brown sugar, and salt until combined. Using a fork, blend in the remaining 8 tablespoons (1 stick) of butter until a crumbly mixture forms. Pour the crumble over the berries.

4. Bake, uncovered, for 35 minutes, or until the berries are bubbling and the crumble is golden brown. Serve warm.

INGREDIENT TIP: Fresh or frozen berries will do the trick in this recipe.

NEW YORK–STYLE
CHEESECAKE

SERVES 8
PREP TIME: 25 minutes, plus 4 hours to chill
COOK TIME: 1 hour 30 minutes, plus 45 minutes to cool
VEGETARIAN, WEEKEND

Thick and decadent, this New York–style cheesecake features the addition of sour cream for a creamier texture. This batter takes minutes to prepare and cooks slowly at low heat to create a dessert that is perfect every time. It is wonderful topped with berry compote or syrup.

4 (8-ounce) packages
   cream cheese, at
   room temperature
1½ cups sugar, plus
   2 tablespoons
5 large eggs
½ cup sour cream
¼ cup all-purpose flour
1 tablespoon
   vanilla extract
1 teaspoon grated
   lemon zest
2 teaspoons freshly
   squeezed lemon juice
½ teaspoon salt, divided
2 cups graham
   cracker crumbs
4 tablespoons (½ stick)
   unsalted butter, melted

1. Position a rack in the middle of the oven and preheat the oven to 325°F. Wrap aluminum foil around the bottom of a 9-inch springform pan, making sure it is tightly wrapped against the sides of the pan. Set aside.

2. In a large bowl, using a handheld mixer, beat together the cream cheese and 1½ cups of sugar until smooth. One at a time, add the eggs, beating after each addition until incorporated.

3. Add the sour cream, flour, vanilla, lemon zest, lemon juice, and ¼ teaspoon of salt. Beat for 2 minutes, or until completely smooth. Set aside.

4. In a small bowl, stir together the graham cracker crumbs, remaining 2 tablespoons of sugar, and remaining ¼ teaspoon of salt.

5. Stir in the melted butter until the cracker mixture is moistened completely. Transfer the cracker mixture to the prepared springform pan and press it into an even layer with the back of a spoon.

6. Pour the cheesecake batter over the crust and set aside.

7. Fill a Dutch oven with 4 cups of water and bring to a boil, then remove from the heat.

8. Carefully place the springform pan into the hot water, then transfer the Dutch oven onto the middle oven rack.

9. Bake, uncovered, for 1 hour. Turn off the oven and leave the cheesecake in the oven with the door closed for 30 minutes. Remove from the oven and let cool for 30 to 45 minutes before wrapping the cheesecake with plastic wrap and refrigerating for at least 4 hours to chill, or overnight.

MAKE-AHEAD TIP: This recipe can be made up to 5 days ahead and kept refrigerated until time to serve. When wrapped well and labeled, the cheesecake can be frozen for up to 4 months.

PINEAPPLE UPSIDE-DOWN CAKE

SERVES 8
PREP TIME: 15 minutes
COOK TIME: 45 minutes, plus 15 minutes to cool
ONE POT, VEGETARIAN

Pineapple upside-down cake is a fun throwback recipe featuring layers of pineapple, cherries, and a buttery moist homemade cake. Flipping the cake upside down to tip it out of the pan means that the sweet pineapple and tart cherries show up on top, making this cake just as good to look at as it is to eat.

1 cup (2 sticks) unsalted butter, at room temperature, divided

¾ cup granulated sugar

¾ cup packed brown sugar, divided

2 large eggs

1 tablespoon vanilla extract

½ cup whole milk

1½ cups all-purpose flour

1½ teaspoons baking powder

¼ teaspoon salt

8 pineapple rings

15 maraschino cherries

½ cup caramel syrup (optional)

1. Preheat the oven to 350°F.

2. In a large bowl, stir together ¾ cup (1½ sticks) of butter, the granulated sugar, ¼ cup of brown sugar, the eggs, and vanilla until smooth. Stir in the milk until blended.

3. Sift in the flour, baking powder, and salt, stirring until just combined.

4. Spread the remaining 4 tablespoons of butter over the bottom of the Dutch oven. Sprinkle the remaining ½ cup of brown sugar over the butter.

5. Arrange the pineapple rings in a single layer on the brown sugar, then place the cherries inside and around the pineapple rings. Carefully pour the batter over the fruit.

6. Bake, uncovered, for 45 minutes, or until a toothpick inserted in the center comes out clean. Remove and let cool for 15 minutes. Place a large platter or plate over the top of the Dutch oven and carefully flip the pot (it is heavy) so the cake is flipped upside down onto the platter with the pineapple and cherries on top. Serve with a drizzle of caramel syrup (if using).

TRIPLE CHOCOLATE CAKE

SERVES 8
PREP TIME: 15 minutes
COOK TIME: 50 minutes
ONE POT, VEGETARIAN

Three distinct type of chocolate combine to build a rich cocoa flavor in this moist cake, decadent enough to serve alone, or it can be topped with whipped cream or your favorite buttercream. It makes a fantastic birthday cake or other celebratory cake to share with friends and family.

2 cups sugar

1½ cups all-purpose flour

¾ cup unsweetened cocoa
   powder, plus more
   for dusting

2 teaspoons
   baking powder

1 teaspoon salt

½ teaspoon
   ground cinnamon

1 cup whole milk

¾ cup vegetable oil

½ cup brewed coffee

½ cup heavy
   (whipping) cream

3 large eggs

1 tablespoon
   vanilla extract

¼ cup semisweet choco-
   late chips, melted

½ cup milk chocolate
   chips, melted

1. Preheat the oven to 350°F. Line a Dutch oven with parchment paper, then lightly coat it with nonstick cooking spray.

2. In a large bowl, sift together the sugar, flour, cocoa powder, baking powder, salt, and cinnamon.

3. In a medium bowl, whisk the milk, oil, coffee, heavy cream, eggs, and vanilla to blend. Add the milk mixture to the dry mixture a little at a time, stirring until just combined.

4. Mix in the melted semisweet chocolate and milk chocolate, then transfer the batter to the prepared Dutch oven.

5. Cover the pot and bake for 30 minutes. Remove the lid and bake for 20 minutes, or until a toothpick inserted in the center comes out clean. Serve hot with a dusting of unsweetened cocoa powder.

VARIATION TIP: If you prefer a slightly sweeter chocolate flavor, omit the semisweet chocolate and replace with milk chocolate.

11

STAPLES

CHICKEN BONE BROTH

MAKES 8 CUPS
PREP TIME: 10 minutes
COOK TIME: 8 hours
DAIRY-FREE, GLUTEN-FREE, ONE POT, WEEKEND

Homemade bone broth is a wonderful way to add flavor to soups and stews, but it also serves as a nutritious supplement to your menu. Cooking this broth in a Dutch oven results in a deep chicken flavor strong enough to stand on its own or to enhance other recipes.

1½ pounds chicken bones
12 cups water
1½ teaspoons salt, plus more as needed
1 teaspoon freshly ground black pepper
4 garlic cloves, peeled
1 lemon, halved
2 tablespoons chopped fresh rosemary leaves
1 tablespoon chopped fresh thyme leaves
1 tablespoon fresh oregano leaves
2 bay leaves

1. Place the chicken bones in a Dutch oven and cover them with the water. Add the salt, pepper, and garlic. Squeeze the juice from the lemon halves into the pot and toss in the rinds. Stir to combine.

2. Bring to a boil over medium heat. Reduce the heat to low and cook for 4 hours, stirring occasionally.

3. Add the rosemary, thyme, oregano, and bay leaves. Cook for 4 hours.

4. Set a strainer over a large heatproof bowl and strain the broth into it. Discard the solids. Taste and season the broth with additional salt, if needed.

5. Serve immediately or store in airtight containers.

MAKE-AHEAD TIP: Keep refrigerated for up to 1 week, or freeze for up to 6 months. When freezing, make sure to leave 1 inch of headspace at the top of the jar or container to allow for expansion.

COUSCOUS

SERVES 6
PREP TIME: 5 minutes
COOK TIME: 10 minutes
ONE POT, VEGAN, WEEKNIGHT

Couscous, a tiny grain-like pasta, makes a wonderful side dish, or it can be added to salads to make them more filling. Preparing couscous with oregano, thyme, and a dash of red pepper brings delicious, versatile flavor to what might otherwise be a bland starch.

1¾ cups Vegetable
　Broth (page 160)
　or store-bought
½ teaspoon
　vegetable bouillon
2 tablespoons extra-virgin
　olive oil
1½ cups couscous
1 teaspoon garlic powder
1 bay leaf
½ teaspoon dried oregano
¼ teaspoon dried thyme
⅛ teaspoon red
　pepper flakes

1. In a Dutch oven over high heat, stir together the broth, vegetable bouillon, and oil and bring to a boil.

2. Stir in the couscous, garlic powder, bay leaf, oregano, thyme, and red pepper flakes. Cover the pot, remove from the heat, and let sit for 5 minutes.

3. Remove and discard the bay leaf. Use a fork to fluff the couscous.

4. Serve immediately or refrigerate in an airtight container for up to 1 week.

INGREDIENT TIP: Replace the vegetable broth with beef broth or chicken broth, if desired.

CREAMY POLENTA

SERVES 4
PREP TIME: 5 minutes
COOK TIME: 30 minutes
GLUTEN-FREE, ONE POT, VEGETARIAN, WEEKNIGHT

Polenta is a delicious, comforting side dish that is easy to make in the Dutch oven because the pot's even heat conduction makes the polenta extra creamy—every time. Here, I enhance that velvety texture with a bit of cream cheese just before serving. This luscious dish pairs wonderfully with Portabella Mushroom Pot Roast (page 86) or Coq au Vin (page 112).

2 cups Vegetable
   Broth (page 160)
   or store-bought
½ cup yellow polenta
1 tablespoon
   unsalted butter
1½ teaspoons salt, plus
   more as needed
2 ounces cream cheese

1. In a Dutch oven over medium heat, bring the broth to a boil. Reduce the heat to low and slowly whisk in the polenta until smooth and completely combined. Stir in the butter and salt.

2. Cover the pot and cook for 22 minutes, stirring occasionally.

3. Remove the Dutch oven from the heat and stir in the cream cheese. Taste and season with additional salt, if needed. Serve immediately.

MAKE-AHEAD TIP: If making ahead, do not add the cream cheese until just before serving.

FLUFFY JASMINE RICE

SERVES 6
PREP TIME: 5 minutes
COOK TIME: 25 minutes
GLUTEN-FREE, ONE POT, VEGAN, WEEKNIGHT

Perfectly cooked rice is one of the first things you should learn to make in your Dutch oven, because it goes with practically anything. Jasmine rice is a long-grain rice with a yummy aroma, and in the Dutch oven, it is ready in about 30 minutes.

1½ cups jasmine rice
3 cups water
1 teaspoon salt

1. Place the rice in a bowl and rinse it under running water until the water runs clear. Drain and set aside.

2. In a Dutch oven over high heat, bring the water to a boil. Add the rice and salt and reduce the heat to low.

3. Cover the pot and simmer for 15 minutes, stirring occasionally to prevent sticking, until tender. If the rice is still firm after 15 minutes, re-cover the pot and let it sit off the heat for 5 minutes more. Fluff the rice with a fork and serve immediately.

MAKE-AHEAD TIP: The rice can be refrigerated for up to 5 days in an airtight container, or frozen for up to 6 months.

GARLIC AND ITALIAN
SAUSAGE BOLOGNESE

MAKES 8 CUPS
PREP TIME: 15 minutes
COOK TIME: 40 minutes
GLUTEN-FREE, ONE POT

Whether you call it Bolognese, pasta sauce, or gravy, this richly seasoned tomato sauce features slightly spicy sausage and a hint of nutmeg and goes well over any type of pasta, sprinkled with some Parmesan cheese.

1 tablespoon extra-virgin olive oil

1 medium white onion, finely diced

1 carrot, finely diced

1 celery stalk, finely diced

4 garlic cloves, minced

1 pound Italian sausage, casings removed

1 cup whole milk

1 (28-ounce) can diced tomatoes

3 tablespoons tomato paste

1 bay leaf

1½ teaspoons Italian seasoning

½ teaspoon salt

½ teaspoon freshly ground black pepper

¼ teaspoon ground nutmeg

1. In a Dutch oven over medium heat, heat the oil. Add the onion, carrot, celery, and garlic and cook for 3 minutes, stirring regularly, until the onion begins to soften.

2. Add the sausage and cook for 5 minutes, stirring regularly, until browned.

3. Add the milk and reduce the heat to low. Simmer for 10 minutes, stirring occasionally.

4. Stir in the tomatoes and their juices, tomato paste, bay leaf, Italian seasoning, salt, pepper, and nutmeg to combine. Simmer for 20 minutes, or until thickened.

VARIATION TIP: If you prefer a milder flavor, use ground beef or ground pork instead of sausage.

TOMATO BASIL

MARINARA SAUCE

MAKES 5 CUPS
PREP TIME: 15 minutes
COOK TIME: 50 minutes
GLUTEN-FREE, ONE POT, VEGAN

Once you make this homemade marinara sauce, you'll never reach for the jarred stuff again. Canned tomatoes pair with fresh basil to create a sauce that is ideal for a basic pasta dish, dipping sauce for bread, or spread over pizza crust.

2 tablespoons extra-virgin olive oil

4 Roma tomatoes, diced

1 small yellow onion, finely diced

4 garlic cloves, minced

1 (28-ounce) can crushed tomatoes

1 cup Vegetable Broth (page 160) or store-bought

2 tablespoons tomato paste

1 tablespoon sugar

1 teaspoon salt

½ cup chopped fresh basil leaves

1. In a Dutch oven over medium heat, heat the oil. Add the Roma tomatoes, onion, and garlic and cook for 5 minutes, stirring regularly, until the onion begins to turn translucent.

2. Stir in the crushed tomatoes, broth, tomato paste, sugar, and salt to combine. Reduce the heat to low, add the basil, and simmer for 40 minutes, stirring occasionally, until thickened.

COOKING TIP: If you prefer a smooth sauce, use an immersion blender after the sauce is done cooking to puree it completely before serving.

VEGETABLE BROTH

MAKES 8 CUPS
PREP TIME: 15 minutes
COOK TIME: 1 hour 30 minutes
GLUTEN-FREE, ONE POT, VEGAN, WEEKEND

Making homemade vegetable broth allows you to create a deep rich flavor you can't find in store-bought options. Packed with flavor and easy to make, this recipe is ideal for use in any soup or stew, or even in recipes like the Creamy Polenta (page 156) or Fluffy Jasmine Rice (page 157) in place of water for extra flavor.

10 cups water

8 ounces carrots, chopped

4 celery stalks, chopped

1 yellow onion, chopped

1 red onion, chopped

1 cup sliced mushrooms

4 garlic cloves, peeled

1 bay leaf

¼ cup chopped
   fresh parsley

1 tablespoon fresh
   thyme leaves

1 teaspoon salt

1. In a Dutch oven over medium heat, combine the water, carrots, celery, yellow and red onions, mushrooms, garlic, bay leaf, parsley, thyme, and salt. Bring to a boil. Reduce the heat to low and simmer, uncovered, for 1½ hours.

2. Place a strainer over a large heatproof bowl and strain the broth in it. Discard the solids. Serve immediately or refrigerate in an airtight container.

INGREDIENT TIP: Collect vegetable peels and scraps as you cook throughout the week and store them in the freezer until you have enough to prepare a batch of broth.

MAKE-AHEAD TIP: Refrigerate the broth for up to 1 week, or freeze for up to 6 months. When freezing, make sure to leave 1 inch of headspace at the top of the jar or container to allow for expansion.

PINTO BEANS

SERVES 8
PREP TIME: 10 minutes
COOK TIME: 2 hours 30 minutes
DAIRY-FREE, GLUTEN-FREE, ONE POT, WEEKEND

Slow-cooked and richly seasoned pinto beans are an excellent source of protein and a nice addition to many meals. I love to serve these beans with a side of Classic Corn Bread (page 37) for a traditional Southern meal.

1 pound dried pinto beans

8 ounces bacon, chopped

1 yellow onion, diced

4 garlic cloves, minced

3 cups water

2 cups Vegetable
Broth (page 160)
or store-bought

1½ teaspoons freshly
ground black pepper

1 teaspoon salt (optional)

1. Wash the pinto beans to remove any bits of dirt and pick through them for any debris.

2. In a Dutch oven over medium heat, cook the bacon for 4 minutes, stirring regularly.

3. Add the onion and garlic and cook for 2 minutes.

4. Add the water, broth, pinto beans, and pepper and bring to a boil.

5. Cover the pot, reduce the heat to low, and cook for about 2 hours, stirring occasionally, until the beans are tender. Taste the beans, and if not tender, continue cooking for 15 to 20 minutes. Taste and add the salt (if using). Serve immediately.

VARIATION TIP: Replace the bacon with pork belly, ham hocks, or 1 tablespoon bacon drippings

MEASUREMENT CONVERSIONS

VOLUME EQUIVALENTS	US STANDARD	US STANDARD (OUNCES)	METRIC (APPROXIMATE)
LIQUID	2 tablespoons	1 fl. oz.	30 mL
	¼ cup	2 fl. oz.	60 mL
	½ cup	4 fl. oz.	120 mL
	1 cup	8 fl. oz.	240 mL
	1½ cups	12 fl. oz.	355 mL
	2 cups or 1 pint	16 fl. oz.	475 mL
	4 cups or 1 quart	32 fl. oz.	1 L
	1 gallon	128 fl. oz.	4 L
DRY	⅛ teaspoon	–	0.5 mL
	¼ teaspoon	–	1 mL
	½ teaspoon	–	2 mL
	¾ teaspoon	–	4 mL
	1 teaspoon	–	5 mL
	1 tablespoon	–	15 mL
	¼ cup	–	59 mL
	⅓ cup	–	79 mL
	½ cup	–	118 mL
	⅔ cup	–	156 mL
	¾ cup	–	177 mL
	1 cup	–	235 mL
	2 cups or 1 pint	–	475 mL
	3 cups	–	700 mL
	4 cups or 1 quart	–	1 L
	½ gallon	–	2 L
	1 gallon	–	4 L

OVEN TEMPERATURES

FAHRENHEIT	CELSIUS (APPROXIMATE)
250°F	120°C
300°F	150°C
325°F	165°C
350°F	180°C
375°F	190°C
400°F	200°C
425°F	220°C
450°F	230°C

WEIGHT EQUIVALENTS

US STANDARD	METRIC (APPROXIMATE)
½ ounce	15 g
1 ounce	30 g
2 ounces	60 g
4 ounces	115 g
8 ounces	225 g
12 ounces	340 g
16 ounces or 1 pound	455 g

REFERENCES

Bush Cooking. "History of Dutch Ovens." Accessed September 30, 2020.
    bushcooking.com/history-dutch-ovens

Beyond the Tent: BeyondtheTent.com

Fresh off the Grid: FreshOfftheGrid.com/camping-recipe-index

INDEX

ACKNOWLEDGMENTS

There are many who influence my life and assist in my daily tasks, but a few played a large part in bringing me to this point and preparing this cookbook for your eyes.

Sister (Stephanie), you shared your love of Dutch ovens with me some time ago, and without that, I would never be here writing this book filled with recipes you helped inspire.

My husband, Larry—you are the best friend I have ever had, and I truly cannot imagine doing life without you. Thank you for always being my willing recipe guinea pig.

Mama and Daddy, I am proud to be your daughter. Thank you for loving me, despite who I have been.

Cathy, my mother-in-law, who has become one of my dearest friends, greatest encouragers, and mentors in faith. Thank you for welcoming me into your life and loving me as your own.

ABOUT THE AUTHOR

Katie Hale started cooking as a child and carried her love of food over to her 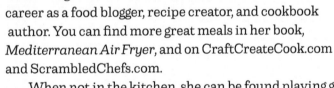 career as a food blogger, recipe creator, and cookbook author. You can find more great meals in her book, *Mediterranean Air Fryer*, and on CraftCreateCook.com and ScrambledChefs.com.

When not in the kitchen, she can be found playing games or watching movies alongside her husband, Larry, and their younger son, Cash. She enjoys weekends at the beaches of Lake Michigan and curling up with a good suspense novel or true crime story.

Her extended family, including her sister, parents, older son Matthew, bonus daughter Megan, granddaughter Aria, and grandson Karson, are her inspirations for creating recipes to share with the world.

CPSIA information can be obtained
at www.ICGtesting.com
Printed in the USA
BVHW021443161021
619025BV00004B/4